THE 6E's OF BRANDING

THE 6E's OF BRANDING

A FRAMEWORK FOR
BRAND STRATEGISTS

MARCOS G. FIGUEIRA

MARCIA BERARDINELLI

The 6E's of Branding: a Framework for Brand Strategists

Copyright © 2024 by Marcos G. Figueira & Marcia Berardinelli.

All rights reserved. No part of this publication may be used in any manner whatsoever without written permission except in the case of brief quotations embodied in critical articles or reviews.

This publication is designed to provide accurate and authoritative in regard to the subject matter covered. While the publisher and author have used their best efforts in preparing this book, they make no representations warranties with respect to the accuracy or completeness of the contents of this book and specifically disclaim any implied warranties of merchantability or fitness for a particular purpose. Neither the publisher nor the author shall be liable for any loss of profit or any other comercial damages, including but not limited to special, incidental, consequential, personal, or other damages.

For information contact: email@marcosfigueira.com
https://marcosfigueira.com

Figueira, Marcos G., & Berardinelli, Marcia.

The 6 E's of Branding: a Framework for Brand Strategists

Edition: 1st ed.

Publication: USA: independently published, 2024.

ISBN: 9798340151155

1. Branding. 2. Brand. 3. Brand Strategy 4. Brand Methodology. 5. Brand Framework. 6. Brand Strategist 7. Brand Building.

TABLE OF CONTENTS

TABLE OF CONTENTS — 5
ABOUT THE 1st AUTHOR — 7
ABOUT THE 2nd AUTHOR — 9
INTRODUCTION — 11
CHAPTER 01 THE FIRST E — 17

Exploration

The role of market research: gathering insights that matter
PEST analysis: understanding the external factors that shape your brand
Semiotic analysis: reading cultural codes to build meaningful brands
Heuristics in branding: How mental shortcuts influence consumer behavior
Competitor audits: finding gaps in the market
Using exploration to discover untapped market potential

CHAPTER 02 THE SECOND E — 45

Essence

What is brand essence? uncovering your brand's true DNA
Naming strategies: how to create a brand name that sticks
Mission, vision, values: aligning your brand's essence with its goals
Personality and tone of voice: crafting a persona customers trust
Brand elasticity: how far can your brand stretch?
A brand that redefined its essence to pivot in the market

CHAPTER 03 THE THIRD E — 71

Expression

The power of storytelling: building emotional connections
From storytelling to storyselling: turning narratives into conversions
Visual identity: building a brand's visual language

Creating brand guidelines: consistency across platforms
Brand voice vs. brand tone: what's the difference?
Building a cohesive brand personality through visual and verbal expression
The role of emotion in brand expression: making people feel, not just think
Brand expression across different platforms

CHAPTER 04 THE FOURTH E   109

Experience

Crafting a seamless brand experience across touchpoints
Sensory branding: Engaging consumers beyond sight and sound
Brand Experience vs. Customer Experience: where the two meet

CHAPTER 05 THE FIFTH E   123

Engagement

The customer journey: Mapping engagement from awareness to advocacy
Customer service as brand engagement: Turning complaints into opportunities.
Community building: how engagement turns customers into brand advocates
Customer retention strategies: keeping your community engaged
Creating a brand community framework: from loyal customers to brand ambassadors

CHAPTER 06 THE SIXTH E   149

Evolution

Brand building strategies: ensuring sustained growth over time
Measuring brand equity: evaluating your brand's market strength
Adapting to market trends: the role of flexibility in brand evolution
Staying relevant: how brands evolve to meet consumer expectations

CONCLUSION   171

The Ongoing Journey Of Brand-Building

Final thoughts on using this framework to future-proof your brand
The power of evolving brands

APPENDIX   175

Branding Glossary

References

THANK YOU   184

ABOUT THE 1ST AUTHOR
Marcos G. Figueira

Marcos Figueira has spent over 30 years devoted to marketing, working across various industries, from finance to publishing, and ultimately finding his passion in growth marketing, performance marketing, and branding. His journey began in the financial sector at **ABN AMRO Bank**, where he honed his marketing skills, before moving to Los Angeles to work in the publishing industry, gaining a deeper understanding of storytelling and brand building.

Since the early 1990s, Marcos has been a partner at **Wyse**, an agency that specializes in growth marketing and strategic branding. Over the years, he has consulted for a wide range of companies, from startups to medium-sized businesses, helping them navigate their growth challenges.

For the past 12 years, Marcos has also shared his knowledge as a professor in MBA programs at Fundação Getúlio Vargas (FGV) in Brazil. With an MBA from PUC, an MSc. from FGV, and a PhD from Rennes Business School in France, his approach to marketing blends practical experience with academic insight.

Currently, Marcos balances his roles as a consultant, speaker, professor, and author. In The 6 E's of Branding, he draws on his experiences to offer straightforward, practical strategies for anyone looking to build their brand. This book isn't about big promises or flashy tricks—it's about sharing what he's learned through years of hands-on work, teaching, and a lot of listening.

ABOUT THE 2ND AUTHOR
Marcia Berardinelli

Marcia Berardinelli is a partner and founder at **Wyse**, a leading marketing consultancy known for helping businesses accelerate growth and scale effectively in today's competitive landscape. With a Master's degree in Customer Experience and a specialization in Growth Marketing, Marcia brings a wealth of knowledge and expertise to every project she undertakes.

Over her career, she has helped hundreds of companies across diverse industries to not only escalate their sales but also build strong, resilient brands. Her approach combines data-driven insights with customer-centric strategies, empowering businesses to optimize their marketing efforts and connect more deeply with their target audiences.

At **Wyse**, Marcia has been at the forefront of the marketing and branding industry's evolution, embracing innovative technologies and growth strategies to deliver measurable results for her clients. She is passionate about transforming the way companies approach growth, always striving to unlock their full potential through a blend of creativity, data, and customer empathy.

As an expert in her field, Marcia shares her insights in this playbook, providing readers with the tools, tactics, and inspiration needed to thrive in the ever-changing world of branding. Whether you're a startup founder, a marketing, branding professional, or a business leader, Marcia's guidance will help you navigate the complexities of branding with confidence and clarity.

INTRODUCTION
why this book will change the way you think about branding

In an increasingly saturated market, brands are no longer just about products and services—they're about experiences, emotions, and identities. Today, standing out requires more than a catchy slogan or a clever logo. It demands a deep connection with consumers, a sharp understanding of the marketplace, and the ability to evolve without losing your essence. This book, *The 6 E's of Branding*, was created to guide you through this new era of brand building, helping you craft a brand that not only captures attention but endures and thrives.

Branding frameworks have been around for decades, and while many of them offer valuable insights, they often fall short in today's rapidly changing landscape. Most frameworks focus on surface-level tactics—visual identity, messaging, or customer targeting—without addressing the full complexity of how brands are built, maintained, and adapted over time. Brands today need more than a one-dimensional approach; they need a holistic strategy that weaves together every aspect of branding, from initial discovery to sustained growth.

That's why *The 6 E's of Branding* was created. This framework fills the gaps left by older methodologies and offers a more comprehensive, actionable approach to branding that keeps pace with the modern market. Unlike traditional models that silo different aspects of branding, the 6 E's provide a unified structure that guides you through each stage of brand building—from the early exploration of market positioning to the ongoing evolution needed to stay relevant in an ever-changing environment.

Filling the gaps: why the 6 E's are different

One of the most widely known frameworks in the branding world is the CORE methodology, which centers on key concepts like clarity, originality, relevance, and endurance. While CORE focuses on creating a distinct and consistent brand identity, it often overlooks the need for adaptability in a fast-paced market. Brands are no longer static entities; they must evolve and respond to trends, customer feedback, and competitive pressures. The 6 E's address this by not only ensuring brands build strong foundations but also by preparing them to adapt, grow, and continuously engage with their audience.

Where frameworks like CORE emphasize building a strong brand identity, they often stop short of explaining how to maintain that identity as the market shifts. The 6 E's take a more dynamic approach. Yes, identity is key (that's where *Essence* comes in), but brands also need to express that identity consistently across all channels (*Expression*), create seamless customer experiences (*Experience*), and, most importantly, evolve (*Evolution*) to remain competitive.

Another well-known model is Marty Neumeier's *ZAG* framework, which emphasizes radical differentiation—"when everyone zigs, you zag." While *ZAG* is excellent for standing out, it can sometimes encourage brands to focus so heavily on differentiation that they lose sight of customer needs. The 6 E's of Branding integrates the importance of uniqueness, but it also stresses the need for a customer-first approach throughout the journey. Differentiation only works if it resonates with the audience, and this framework ensures that by the time you express your brand, you've already done the deep work of understanding who your customers are and what they care about.

Why this book matters now

The digital age has fundamentally changed the way consumers interact with brands. Today's customers are hyper-informed, ultra-connected, and expect more from the companies they support. They want to feel a connection to the brands they choose, and they expect those brands to reflect their values, offer more than just a product, and respond to societal changes in real-time.

With social media, e-commerce, and the rise of online reviews, customers have more influence than ever before, which means your brand is being shaped by your customers as much as by your marketing team. This requires a new level of agility in brand building—one that goes beyond traditional marketing techniques and dives into creating authentic, emotional connections.

Traditional branding frameworks often fail to address these complexities. Many of them are rooted in an era when the market was slower, and consumer expectations were simpler. In contrast, *The 6 E's of Branding* was designed with the modern marketer in mind. It doesn't just tell you how to create a logo or a tagline; it walks you through how to discover your brand's unique *Essence*, how to create a cohesive *Experience* across every touchpoint, and how to engage your customers in ways that build lasting loyalty.

What's more, this framework emphasizes the importance of brand *Evolution*—recognizing that the work of branding never stops. The brands that succeed in the long term are those that continuously adapt to changing consumer needs, market trends, and technological advancements. This is what makes the 6 E's so critical for today's brands. It doesn't just help you create a strong brand identity—it helps you future-proof that identity by equipping you with the tools to adapt and grow.

How the 6 E's fill in the gaps left by other frameworks

Other branding models have given us useful concepts, but they often operate in silos. The 6 E's of Branding offers an integrated framework that acknowledges branding as a dynamic, ongoing process. Let's break down how it fills the gaps:

- **Exploration**: Where many frameworks assume you know your market and your audience, this book begins with an in-depth discovery process. Understanding your competitors, market gaps, and untapped opportunities ensures you start with a clear direction.

- **Essence**: This is your brand's DNA—its purpose, personality, and values. While other models touch on identity, the 6 E's ensure that you don't just create an identity, but you anchor it in what your brand truly stands for.

- **Expression**: A cohesive and authentic brand expression goes beyond logos and colors. It's about how your brand communicates its identity across every platform, voice, and visual element.

- **Experience**: Many frameworks neglect the experience part of branding, assuming that a strong identity is enough. But in a customer-driven world, the experience at every touchpoint is crucial. The 6 E's guide you through creating a seamless and meaningful brand experience.

- **Engagement**: While most frameworks offer some version of customer interaction, the 6 E's focus on building real relationships. Engagement isn't just about marketing; it's about creating a community and turning customers into advocates.

- **Evolution**: This final piece is where most frameworks stop. *The 6 E's of Branding* recognizes that branding is not static. To stay relevant, brands must evolve. This book gives you the tools to anticipate market changes, innovate, and grow without losing your core identity.

Future-proofing your brand with the 6 E's

This book isn't just about building a brand for today—it's about creating a brand that can stand the test of time. By understanding how to evolve, engage, and remain authentic to your brand's core values, you'll be equipped to handle whatever changes come your way, whether they're driven by technological advances, cultural shifts, or new competitors.

The 6 E's of Branding offers a holistic, flexible approach that goes beyond what other frameworks provide. It's for anyone serious about building a brand that doesn't just make noise in the marketplace but creates lasting connections and remains adaptable as the world changes. Whether you're an entrepreneur launching a new brand or a seasoned marketer looking to refine an established one, this book provides the roadmap you need to future-proof your brand for long-term success.

The 6 E's of Branding Model

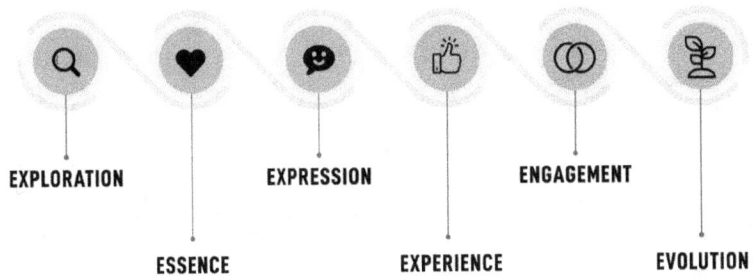

CHAPTER 01
THE FIRST E

Exploration

The role of market research: gathering insights that matter

In a world flooded with brands vying for attention, standing out has never been more critical — or more challenging. The temptation is often to jump straight into the exciting stuff: crafting logos, developing campaigns, and rolling out products. But before a brand can even think about how it looks or sounds, it needs to understand one vital truth: without market research, you're building your brand on guesswork. And guessing, in the world of branding, is a gamble most businesses can't afford to take.

Market research isn't just about gathering facts and figures. It's the foundation of a strong, strategic brand, the compass that keeps you heading in the right direction. Whether you're a new brand trying to carve out a niche or an established name seeking to stay relevant, knowing the lay of the land is everything. This process starts with asking the right questions: What does your market look like? Who are your competitors? What do your customers really want, even if they can't articulate it yet?

Market research is a lot like detective work. You're sifting through clues—data, trends, consumer behavior—looking for patterns and insights that can guide you. But unlike detectives, who often chase after "whodunit" answers, your goal is to understand "what's next?" for your brand. And it all begins with a deep dive into the market you want to serve.

Understanding your customers: more than just numbers

One of the biggest misconceptions about market research is that it's all about the numbers. Sales figures, demographic data, income brackets—sure, these are important, but they're just the tip of the iceberg. Real market research digs deeper, going beyond spreadsheets and pie charts. It's about understanding not only who your customers are but why they make the decisions they do. What motivates them? What problems do they face that your brand can solve? And perhaps most crucially: what are they not telling you?

The famous American marketing professor Philip Kotler once said, "The best advertising is done by satisfied customers." But before you can satisfy a customer, you need to know them better than they know themselves. This is where qualitative research—focus groups, interviews, customer reviews—comes in. When you sit down and listen to people's stories, frustrations, and desires, patterns start to emerge that no survey could ever capture.

For example, a local gym might see in their demographic data that their average member is in their early 30s. But after conducting qualitative interviews, they find that many members are also young parents looking for quick, effective workouts that fit into their hectic schedules. This insight might lead the gym to introduce express classes during lunch hours or offer child-friendly programs, helping them address a pain point that wasn't obvious in the raw data.

Competitor analysis: knowing where you stand

Once you understand your customers, the next logical step is to turn your focus outward: to your competitors. This isn't just about knowing who they are—it's about figuring out what they're doing right, and more importantly, what they're getting wrong. A well-executed competitor analysis allows you to pinpoint gaps in the market, areas where your brand can step in and offer something unique.

It's tempting to look at the big players in your industry and assume you should emulate their success. After all, if they're thriving, it must mean they've cracked the code, right? Not necessarily. Sometimes, the most valuable insights come from identifying what competitors overlook. Is there a segment of the market they're ignoring? A customer need they're failing to address? These are the sweet spots where your brand can thrive.

A great example of this is Netflix in its early days. When Blockbuster was the dominant player in the movie rental industry, Netflix didn't try to out-Blockbuster them. Instead, they identified a pain point—customers hated late fees—and built their entire business model around removing that frustration. They didn't compete on convenience or location; they competed on customer experience. We all know how that story ended.

Trends and shifts: riding the wave

Markets are living, breathing entities. They shift, change, and evolve, often in ways that can feel unpredictable. But if you've done your homework, you can spot emerging trends before they hit the mainstream—and this is where market research becomes your most powerful tool.

The trick is to not just react to trends but to anticipate them. In today's fast-paced digital world, customers are constantly bombarded with new ideas, products, and services. Brands that can tap into a trend at the right moment—not too early, not too late—are the ones that ride the wave to success. And this takes more than just paying attention to what's trending on social media. It requires a deeper understanding of cultural shifts, economic forces, and technological advancements.

Take the rise of sustainability as a business trend. For years, it was something only a niche group of consumers cared about. But as the global conversation around climate change grew louder, the demand for sustainable products exploded. Brands like Patagonia were able to ride that wave because they'd already woven environmental responsibility into their brand DNA, long before it became fashionable. That's the power of seeing where the market is headed — and preparing for it.

Avoiding the trap of over-researching

While research is undeniably crucial, it's easy to fall into the trap of endless analysis. You can spend months, even years, gathering data, but there comes a point where you need to stop researching and start acting. The goal of market research is to inform your decisions, not to paralyze them.

Too much analysis can lead to what's often called "paralysis by analysis" — that overwhelming feeling that you need just one more report or one more customer interview before you can take the plunge. In truth, no amount of research will give you a 100% guarantee of success. What it does offer is a solid foundation on which to build, giving you confidence that you're making informed, strategic decisions rather than shooting in the dark.

So, while research is your brand's best friend, it's not a substitute for action. The trick is to gather enough insight to feel confident about your direction, and then move forward, knowing that your understanding of the market will evolve along the way.

In branding, as in life, knowledge is power. But the real power comes from what you do with that knowledge.

PEST analysis: understanding the external factors that shape your brand

Building a brand in today's volatile market is like sailing through an unpredictable sea. You might have the perfect ship—your brand's identity, values, and products—but without a clear understanding of the weather patterns (the external environment), you're setting yourself up for a rough journey. This is where PEST analysis comes in. It's your radar system, helping you navigate the waters by understanding the forces that can affect your brand in the long term.

PEST analysis breaks down the macro-environmental factors that can shape a brand into four categories: Political, Economic, Social, and Technological. These are not things you can control directly, but understanding them allows you to anticipate changes, adapt quickly, and capitalize on emerging opportunities.

Let's explore how each of these elements influences your brand and how you can leverage this knowledge to stay ahead of the curve.

Political factors: navigating the regulatory minefield

Politics may not be the first thing that comes to mind when you think about branding, but it's impossible to ignore. Political decisions shape the playing field for businesses, from taxation to trade policies, labor laws, and environmental regulations. Whether you're a local startup or a global brand, changes in government policy can dramatically impact how you operate.

For example, think about the strict regulations on data privacy that emerged with the introduction of the General Data Protection Regulation (GDPR) in the European Union. Companies around the world had to scramble to ensure compliance with these new rules, revamping their data handling processes or risking massive fines. But brands that were ahead of the curve, prepared for these political shifts, turned this challenge into an opportunity—showing customers that they were serious about privacy and transparency.

When conducting a PEST analysis, you should ask: What current or upcoming legislation could affect your business? Is there political instability in the regions where you operate? Are there changes in international trade agreements that could influence your supply chain? By paying attention to these political winds, you can sail smoothly through storms that might sink less prepared competitors.

Economic factors: riding the market's ups and downs

Economies are like the ocean tides—constantly rising and falling. While businesses can't control these tides, they can learn to ride them. Economic conditions influence consumer spending, interest rates, inflation, and employment levels, all of which have a direct impact on your brand.

Take the 2008 financial crisis, for example. It was a seismic event that saw consumer confidence plummet and companies across industries struggle. Yet, brands like Apple continued to thrive during the recession. Why? Because they understood that during tough economic times, consumers become more selective about where they spend their money. Apple focused on maintaining its premium positioning and strong customer loyalty, offering products that felt worth the investment even when budgets were tight.

In your PEST analysis, consider questions like: What's the current economic outlook in the markets you serve? Are we heading toward inflation or a recession? How do fluctuations in exchange rates or interest rates affect your bottom line? Understanding these economic variables allows you to adjust pricing strategies, product offerings, and even marketing messages to match the financial mood of your audience.

Social factors: decoding the human side of the market

Social factors might be the most dynamic and fast-changing element in the PEST analysis, and they hold immense power over a brand's relevance. Consumer attitudes, lifestyle shifts, cultural norms, and social values evolve over time, often quicker than brands anticipate. Brands that fail to keep up with these social currents risk becoming outdated or even irrelevant.

One of the most famous examples of a brand successfully riding a social wave is Dove's **"Real Beauty" campaign**. Launched in 2004, Dove tapped into the growing societal demand for authenticity and self-acceptance in a world obsessed with perfection. The campaign, which featured real women instead of airbrushed models, resonated deeply with consumers and helped Dove position itself as a champion of body positivity. It wasn't just a marketing move—it was a reflection of the shifting social attitudes around beauty standards.

When analyzing social factors, think about your audience's evolving expectations. Are there generational changes affecting your customer base? How do shifts in work-life balance, health consciousness, or environmental awareness impact your product or service? Brands that connect with social trends on a deeper level create not just customers, but communities.

For example, consider the rise of eco-conscious consumers. Brands like Patagonia and Tesla have thrived because they embraced the environmental concerns of their audience, integrating sustainability into their core values long before it became a mainstream demand. Now, sustainability isn't just a trend; it's a key differentiator for brands aiming to build long-term loyalty.

Technological factors: staying ahead of innovation

In today's world, technology doesn't just change industries—it disrupts them entirely. Staying on top of technological advances isn't optional; it's a necessity. From artificial intelligence to e-commerce platforms, blockchain to social media algorithms, brands must be ready to adapt to the constantly evolving technological landscape.

Look at how Netflix disrupted the movie rental industry. Blockbuster had the market cornered with its brick-and-mortar stores, but when Netflix leveraged emerging technologies—first through DVD-by-mail services, and later through streaming—it not only upended Blockbuster's business model but also changed how the world consumes entertainment. Brands that fail to embrace technological change, like Blockbuster, quickly find themselves obsolete.

In your PEST analysis, ask yourself: What technological trends could disrupt your industry? Are there new tools that could improve your customer experience or streamline your operations? How will emerging technologies like AI, augmented reality, or 5G networks change the way consumers interact with your brand?

Take a brand like Warby Parker, which revolutionized the eyewear market by embracing e-commerce and virtual try-ons, effectively removing the need for physical stores. By adopting new technologies, they were able to offer something unique and build a loyal customer base in a market dominated by established players.

Putting PEST analysis into action: a holistic view

PEST analysis isn't something you do once and then put on the shelf. It's a living, breathing process that should evolve as the external environment changes. The real value of PEST analysis comes when it's used proactively—allowing your brand to anticipate challenges and seize opportunities before competitors even know they exist.

For example, consider the rise of remote work due to the COVID-19 pandemic. Brands that were quick to adapt their operations and marketing strategies to this new reality—such as offering home office products or tailoring services for at-home consumers—were able to thrive during a time of massive disruption. Those that hesitated or ignored these external factors struggled to stay afloat.

By understanding the political, economic, social, and technological factors that shape your market, your brand isn't just reacting to changes—it's evolving with them. This is what separates the brands that survive from those that thrive.

The next time you're planning a major brand strategy, think of PEST as your crystal ball. It won't give you all the answers, but it will shine a light on the trends, challenges, and opportunities waiting on the horizon, helping your brand chart a course for success.

Semiotic analysis: reading cultural codes to build meaningful brands

Every brand tells a story, but not all stories are heard or understood the way we intend. Why does one logo trigger immediate recognition and loyalty, while another fades into the background? How can a tagline resonate deeply with one culture but miss the mark in another? The answers to these questions lie in the world of semiotics — the study of signs and symbols, and how we interpret them. Brands that tap into the power of semiotic analysis can decode the cultural cues that influence their audiences, ensuring their messaging not only lands but sticks.

Semiotics isn't some abstract academic theory reserved for philosophers and linguists. It's an incredibly practical tool for brands, allowing them to craft visuals, language, and experiences that speak directly to the subconscious of their target audience. At its core, semiotic analysis helps brands understand the deep, often unspoken, cultural codes that shape how people perceive the world around them. In a globalized marketplace, where brands are increasingly vying for the attention of diverse audiences, mastering these codes is the key to creating meaningful connections.

The power of symbols: logos, colors, and beyond

Take a moment and picture the logo of Nike: a simple swoosh. It's not just a piece of graphic design — it's a symbol that has come to embody movement, athleticism, and victory. This transformation didn't happen overnight. Through years of carefully crafted brand messaging, Nike's swoosh has become a universal signifier of aspiration and athletic excellence. The brand tapped into cultural values surrounding sports, competition, and achievement, and embedded those ideas into their visual identity.

This is the essence of semiotics in branding. Logos, colors, fonts, and imagery all carry cultural meanings that go beyond their immediate aesthetic value. When brands understand the cultural associations attached to these elements, they can build visual identities that resonate on a deeper emotional level. For example, the color red often symbolizes energy, passion, or even danger in Western cultures, but it can evoke prosperity and good fortune in many Asian cultures. A brand that wants to launch in multiple global markets must consider these associations or risk sending the wrong message.

A classic case of semiotic misalignment happened when Pepsi altered its logo in South East Asia in the 1950s. They changed the dominant color from deep blue to light blue, unaware that light blue is a color associated with mourning and death in that region. The new branding was a disaster, and Pepsi had to revert to its original design. This misstep underscores the importance of understanding the cultural significance of symbols before rolling out a global campaign.

Language as a cultural signifier

Semiotics isn't just about logos and colors—it's also about the language we use. Words themselves are cultural symbols, and the meanings they carry can shift dramatically depending on context. Think of the word "home." For some, it might conjure images of warmth, family, and security, while for others, it might evoke a sense of confinement or isolation. A brand that uses the term "home" in its messaging must be acutely aware of the emotional and cultural baggage that comes with it.

Language is full of these kinds of hidden signals, and brands that ignore them can find themselves unintentionally alienating their audience. Consider how Dove's "Real Beauty" campaign flipped traditional beauty language on its head. Rather than pushing aspirational but often unattainable ideals, Dove's language celebrated real, everyday beauty. Words like "natural," "authentic," and "self-love" became central to the brand's messaging, aligning perfectly with the growing cultural shift toward body positivity and self-acceptance.

This linguistic shift wasn't accidental—it was a response to deep cultural changes in how society views beauty standards. Dove tapped into the semiotic landscape, reading the signals of a changing world, and positioned itself as a champion of this new, more inclusive narrative.

Decoding cultural narratives: understanding the context

One of the most powerful aspects of semiotic analysis is its ability to help brands tap into broader cultural narratives. Every society has its myths, archetypes, and stories that shape how people see themselves and the world. These narratives are often so deeply embedded in our culture that we don't even realize they exist—but they heavily influence how we interpret brands.

For example, in the West, there is a strong cultural narrative around individualism. This idea—the notion of standing out, forging your own path, and rejecting conformity—has shaped countless brand identities, from Harley-Davidson to Apple. These brands tap into the archetype of the rebel, the maverick who breaks the rules to create something new. Harley-Davidson's entire brand is built on the idea of freedom and rebellion, selling not just motorcycles but a lifestyle that rejects the ordinary and embraces the open road.

Contrast this with many Asian cultures, where collectivism is a more dominant narrative. Brands in these markets often focus on harmony, community, and respect for tradition. A successful brand in Japan or South Korea might emphasize family values or the importance of contributing to society, rather than focusing on individual achievement.

Applying semiotics to brand storytelling

Storytelling is at the heart of branding, and semiotic analysis offers brands the tools to tell stories that resonate across different cultural contexts. A brand story isn't just a series of events — it's a collection of signs and symbols that communicate meaning to the audience. By using semiotics, brands can ensure that their stories align with the cultural codes and values of their target market.

Let's look at Patagonia as a case in point. The outdoor apparel brand has built its entire identity around environmental activism and sustainability. Every element of Patagonia's storytelling, from its product design to its marketing campaigns, taps into the cultural narrative of environmentalism. This narrative is particularly powerful in today's world, where climate change and sustainable living are top-of-mind issues for many consumers. By aligning itself with this cultural shift, Patagonia doesn't just sell clothing — it sells a philosophy, a commitment to preserving the planet.

The brand's use of semiotics extends beyond its marketing. Its logo — a simple mountain range — communicates adventure, nature, and endurance, all values that align with its environmental message. Patagonia has successfully embedded itself into the culture of outdoor enthusiasts and eco-conscious consumers, becoming more than just a brand; it's a movement.

The risks of ignoring semiotics

Brands that ignore the power of semiotics risk sending mixed or even harmful messages. A famous case of semiotic failure occurred with the luxury brand Dolce & Gabbana in 2018. The brand launched a campaign in China featuring a Chinese model struggling to eat Italian food with chopsticks. The campaign was intended to be playful, but it was widely seen as disrespectful and ignorant of Chinese culture, triggering a massive backlash. What Dolce & Gabbana failed to grasp was the deep cultural pride surrounding Chinese traditions, including the use of chopsticks. The brand's inability to understand these cultural symbols cost it credibility and, ultimately, market share.

In another example, when HSBC launched its "Assume Nothing" campaign in the early 2000s, it found that the tagline didn't translate well in many Asian markets. The concept of "assuming nothing" clashed with the cultural value placed on trust and certainty. HSBC had to overhaul the entire campaign to better fit the cultural context of its global markets.

These examples illustrate the dangers of ignoring semiotics or assuming that symbols, words, and images will be interpreted the same way across cultures. Brands that fail to do their homework risk alienating entire markets and damaging their reputation.

Semiotics as a strategic tool

Incorporating semiotic analysis into your brand strategy is about more than just avoiding pitfalls—it's about creating meaningful, culturally resonant brands that connect with audiences on a deeper level. Whether you're launching a new product, rebranding, or entering a new market, semiotics offers a roadmap for ensuring that your messaging aligns with the cultural codes of your audience.

At its heart, branding is about meaning. And meaning is shaped by culture. By understanding the signs, symbols, and narratives that define your target market, you can build a brand that doesn't just communicate—it connects.

Heuristics in branding: How mental shortcuts influence consumer behavior

Have you ever found yourself reaching for a product without thinking twice, maybe that same coffee brand you always grab or the sneakers you keep repurchasing? Chances are, you weren't weighing pros and cons or doing a cost-benefit analysis—your brain took a shortcut. These mental shortcuts, known as heuristics, play a huge role in shaping consumer behavior. They are the cognitive tools we rely on to make quick decisions in an overwhelming marketplace.

For brands, understanding heuristics is like unlocking the secret code to consumer minds. When brands design their strategies with these mental shortcuts in mind, they make it easier for customers to choose them over the competition. From pricing strategies to packaging design, brands that tap into these automatic decision-making processes can gain a huge advantage.

What are heuristics?

In the simplest terms, heuristics are mental shortcuts our brains use to simplify decision-making. Instead of spending time analyzing every option, we rely on familiar cues—like price, brand reputation, or social proof—to guide our choices. This is especially true in fast-paced environments where consumers are bombarded with choices and information.

For instance, if you're deciding which toothpaste to buy, you likely don't read the ingredients on each package or compare every price point. Instead, you go with the brand you've always used, the one that's on sale, or the one with the coolest packaging. That's heuristics in action.

Psychologists Amos Tversky and Daniel Kahneman, who pioneered research on heuristics, showed that people make decisions based on cognitive biases rather than rational analysis. These mental shortcuts allow us to process information quickly, but they also make us vulnerable to influences that brands can exploit—both consciously and subconsciously.

The familiarity heuristic: the power of brand recognition

One of the most powerful heuristics in branding is the familiarity heuristic, also known as the "mere-exposure effect." It's the idea that people are more likely to choose something simply because they've seen it before. Familiarity breeds trust. This is why brands spend millions on repetitive advertising. The more you see a logo or hear a jingle, the more comfortable you feel with the brand. Over time, you associate that brand with safety, reliability, and ease of choice, even if you haven't consciously engaged with it.

Take Coca-Cola, for example. You may not actively think about your preference for Coke over Pepsi, but years of exposure to Coca-Cola's branding—from TV ads to billboards and packaging—have made it a default choice for many people. When you're standing in front of the fridge at a convenience store, your brain doesn't have to think much—it sees the familiar red and white label and makes the decision for you. That's the familiarity heuristic at work.

Brands looking to build this kind of instinctual loyalty need to focus on consistency in their messaging, visual identity, and presence. The more familiar your brand becomes in the minds of consumers, the easier it is for them to choose you without a second thought.

The price heuristic: how consumers link cost with value

Another common mental shortcut is the price heuristic, where consumers assume that higher-priced products are of higher quality. This is why luxury brands like Rolex or Gucci can charge astronomical prices. People don't just buy the product—they buy the perception of value that comes with it. The price acts as a signal, telling the consumer, "This is special. This is worth it."

This heuristic can work both ways. For instance, brands that compete on price often use discounts and "limited-time offers" to trigger another kind of price-related shortcut—the idea that they're getting a great deal. Think of Black Friday sales. Consumers flock to stores, often buying items they don't need, simply because they see a slashed price and feel like they're getting a bargain.

In branding, mastering the price heuristic means understanding how your pricing strategy communicates value. Are you positioning your brand as a luxury offering? If so, your price should reflect that—consumers expect to pay more for premium products. On the other hand, if you want to build a brand known for affordability, emphasizing discounts, promotions, and "bang-for-buck" messaging will make it easier for consumers to justify their purchase.

The scarcity heuristic: limited availability creates urgency

The scarcity heuristic is another tool brands frequently use to influence consumer decisions. When something feels scarce—whether it's time-limited, low in stock, or part of an exclusive release—people place higher value on it. It's the fear of missing out, or FOMO, in action.

One of the most iconic uses of the scarcity heuristic comes from Nike's limited-edition sneaker drops. When Nike releases a new pair of Air Jordans in a limited quantity, the rush to buy them isn't just about the product—it's about getting your hands on something rare. This scarcity creates a sense of urgency and heightens the perceived value, turning the product into a coveted item.

Scarcity can also apply to services or experiences. Brands in the travel industry, like airlines or booking platforms, frequently use the scarcity heuristic with messages like, "Only 2 seats left at this price" or "Rooms filling up fast." Even if the customer wasn't planning to book right away, the fear of missing out on a deal or a rare opportunity nudges them toward making a decision.

To effectively use the scarcity heuristic, brands must walk a fine line between creating urgency and being genuine. If customers feel like scarcity is artificial or manipulative, it can damage trust. But when used appropriately, scarcity can transform a product or service from something nice-to-have into a must-have.

Social proof: the shortcut of following the crowd

Humans are social creatures, and one of the most persuasive heuristics is social proof. This mental shortcut is rooted in the idea that if other people like something, it must be good. We look to the behavior of others to inform our decisions, especially when we're unsure of what to do.

This is why customer reviews, testimonials, and influencer endorsements have become so crucial in branding. When you see thousands of five-star reviews on Amazon or watch your favorite influencer rave about a skincare product on Instagram, your brain takes a shortcut: if they like it, it's probably worth buying.

Brands like Glossier have mastered this strategy. Glossier doesn't just sell makeup—they sell social proof. Their user-generated content model invites customers to share their own makeup looks, reviews, and experiences, creating a community where consumers feel validated in their choices because they see real people just like them using the products.

Incorporating social proof into your branding means highlighting customer stories, showcasing reviews, and building communities that encourage interaction and trust. The more your audience sees others engaging with your brand, the more likely they are to follow suit.

The authority heuristic: trust through expertise

The authority heuristic is all about expertise. When a brand is seen as an expert in its field, people are more likely to trust and buy from it. Think about how Apple is perceived in the tech world. Despite the availability of cheaper alternatives, people continue to buy iPhones, largely because of Apple's reputation as a leader in innovation. The brand's authority in the technology space creates a mental shortcut for consumers—if Apple makes it, it must be top-notch.

This is why so many brands leverage endorsements from experts, professionals, or industry certifications. When consumers see that a product is backed by a trusted figure or organization, they're more likely to believe in its quality without doing extensive research themselves.

For your brand, establishing authority might mean emphasizing awards, certifications, or expert opinions. The goal is to build credibility so that when consumers see your name, their brains automatically equate it with expertise and trustworthiness.

Using heuristics to build brand loyalty

At the heart of all these heuristics is the idea of making things easier for the consumer. In a world full of choices, consumers don't want to sift through every option—they want their decisions to feel simple and justified. Brands that align with these mental shortcuts make life easier for their customers, fostering loyalty in the process.

Heuristics can be particularly powerful for brand building because they create instinctive connections with consumers. A customer might not consciously know why they chose your product, but if your branding has effectively tapped into their subconscious through familiarity, price, scarcity, or social proof, they'll feel confident in their choice.

Ultimately, heuristics allow brands to do more than just sell—they allow brands to become the default choice. And once a brand reaches that level of ingrained trust and ease, it moves from being just another option to being the only option in the consumer's mind.

Competitor audits: finding gaps in the market

Every market is a battlefield. To succeed, you need to know not just your customers, but also your competitors. A competitor audit is like reconnaissance for your brand—it's the process of assessing your competition, not just to see what they're doing right, but to uncover what they're missing. Done well, a competitor audit reveals the white spaces—the gaps in the market where your brand can shine.

Too many brands fall into the trap of copying their competitors, convinced that if it worked for someone else, it'll work for them. But playing catch-up is no way to stand out. A competitor audit isn't about imitation; it's about differentiation. It's a process of looking at the strengths and weaknesses of others to better position your brand for success. It's not enough to know who your competitors are—you need to know their blind spots and how to turn those into your opportunities.

Knowing who you're up against

The first step in any competitor audit is identifying your direct and indirect competitors. Direct competitors are those offering a similar product or service to the same market. They're often the brands we're most focused on because they're fighting for the same customers. But indirect competitors can be just as crucial to understand. These are brands that may offer a different product but solve the same problem for your customers. For instance, Netflix and YouTube are indirect competitors—they're not offering the same service, but both compete for your audience's time and attention.

Once you've identified your competitors, it's time to dive deep into their brands. What's their positioning? What's their messaging? How do they engage with customers? These questions are critical because they help you understand not just what your competitors do, but how they communicate who they are.

For example, let's say you're launching a new coffee brand. Your direct competitors are obvious: Starbucks, Dunkin', and local coffee shops. But your indirect competitors could include tea companies, energy drink brands, or even health and wellness products that promise to boost energy. Understanding this broader landscape allows you to see the market holistically, helping you spot where your brand can offer something different.

Identifying strengths and weaknesses

Every competitor has its strengths, but it's the weaknesses that offer the most insight. The goal of a competitor audit is to find those weaknesses and exploit them—not by undercutting them directly, but by offering something they don't. Maybe your competitors are focused on premium pricing, but their customer service is lacking. Or perhaps they've nailed their online presence but have weak in-store experiences. Every flaw is an opportunity.

For instance, think of Warby Parker, the eyewear brand. When they launched, the eyewear market was dominated by high-end brands like Luxottica, which controlled much of the market through exclusive retail agreements and inflated prices. Warby Parker identified a significant gap—there was no affordable, stylish option for consumers who didn't want to pay hundreds of dollars for glasses. They positioned themselves as the disruptors, offering sleek, affordable eyewear with a socially conscious mission. Their competitor audit allowed them to zero in on the weaknesses of the big players—price and accessibility—and capitalize on them.

When conducting your own competitor audit, ask yourself: where do my competitors fall short? Is it customer service? Product variety? Speed of delivery? By identifying these pain points, you can position your brand as the solution.

Filling the gaps: what are they missing?

Finding gaps in the market is more art than science. It's about looking for the places where your competitors either aren't serving their customers well or aren't serving them at all. These gaps might be obvious, like a lack of eco-friendly products in a market that's increasingly sustainability-conscious. Or they might be subtle, like the emotional tone of your competitors' messaging. Do all your competitors speak with the same polished, corporate voice? Maybe there's room for a brand that feels more human, more authentic.

Consider the skincare industry. For years, the market was dominated by brands like Clinique and Olay, known for their clinical, science-backed approaches to skincare. But in recent years, brands like Glossier and The Ordinary have skyrocketed by focusing on transparency and a community-driven approach. Glossier's competitor audit likely revealed that while the big players were seen as experts, they felt distant and inaccessible. By focusing on relatable, everyday beauty and engaging directly with consumers through social media, Glossier filled the emotional gap that the legacy brands had left open.

Gaps in the market can also be technological. Think about Uber and how they disrupted the transportation industry. Taxis had a stronghold for decades, but the experience was often frustrating—long wait times, inconsistent pricing, and a lack of convenience. Uber's audit of the taxi industry would have highlighted these issues. The gap they filled wasn't just about price or service; it was about creating a seamless user experience through technology. With a tap of a button, you could hail a ride, track your driver, and pay—all without fumbling for cash. Uber didn't reinvent the wheel; they just found the gaps in an outdated system and filled them with innovation.

Keeping an eye on future threats

Competitor audits aren't static; they're dynamic. The market is constantly evolving, and new competitors can appear seemingly out of nowhere. That's why it's important to treat competitor analysis as an ongoing process, not a one-time task. Just because a competitor isn't on your radar now doesn't mean they won't be a threat in the future.

Consider Blockbuster in the early 2000s. At its peak, Blockbuster was the undisputed king of movie rentals, with thousands of stores across the U.S. But they failed to take Netflix seriously as a competitor. Netflix, at the time, was still a mail-order DVD rental company, a blip on Blockbuster's radar. Blockbuster's failure to see

Netflix as a future threat cost them dearly when Netflix pivoted to streaming and revolutionized the industry.

By keeping an eye on emerging competitors and trends, you can anticipate changes in your market and be ready to adjust your strategy. It's not enough to just look at the competitors who are doing well now—you need to think about who might come up behind you. Are there startups in your space experimenting with new technologies? Are consumer behaviors shifting in ways that could give rise to new players? Staying alert to these shifts can give your brand a competitive advantage, allowing you to pivot before your competitors even see the threat.

Building your brand's unique positioning

Once you've completed your competitor audit, the final step is turning those insights into action. How can your brand stand out in a crowded market? What's your unique value proposition that sets you apart from the competition? Maybe it's offering a better price, but more often, it's about delivering something that your competitors can't or won't.

Your brand's positioning should be a direct reflection of the gaps you've identified in the market. If your competitors are all focused on premium products, maybe there's room for a brand that's more accessible. If they're all focused on functionality, perhaps you can emphasize aesthetics or emotional connection. The key is to carve out a space that is authentically yours—a space where your brand can not only survive but thrive.

Think of Airbnb. When it launched, the hotel industry was a monolith, and the idea of staying in a stranger's home seemed crazy to most people. But Airbnb identified a gap—a growing desire among travelers for more authentic, local experiences—and turned it into a billion-dollar business. They didn't try to compete with hotels on luxury or convenience; instead, they offered something entirely different: the feeling of living like a local, with a unique and personal touch. This gap allowed them to redefine the travel industry.

In the end, a competitor audit isn't just about knowing where you stand—it's about finding the spaces where your competitors aren't standing at all. It's about looking at the market from a bird's-eye view, identifying the opportunities others have missed, and making them your own. That's how brands don't just survive but lead.

Using exploration to discover untapped market potential

In the world of branding, the difference between success and failure often comes down to seeing what others miss. Markets are full of noise—endless brands, countless messages, and an overwhelming array of options for consumers. So, how does a brand stand out in such a crowded environment? The answer lies in exploration, in doing the work to dig deeper than the competition. This is where untapped market potential lives—hidden in consumer needs that are overlooked, in gaps competitors have ignored, or in trends just starting to take shape. For brands willing to invest in exploration, the rewards can be game-changing.

Exploration in branding isn't just about data; it's about curiosity and the willingness to question assumptions. Brands that take the time to look beyond the obvious and challenge industry norms often find themselves in territory no one else has thought to claim. This process requires a mix of market research, competitor analysis, and a keen understanding of emerging cultural or technological trends.

Let's take a look at how exploration has helped brands discover new opportunities and break into untapped markets.

The power of listening to your customers

The first step in exploration is always listening—really listening—to your customers. This isn't about skimming online reviews or sending out generic surveys. It's about engaging with people on a deeper level, understanding their unspoken needs and frustrations. Often, customers don't even realize what they want until a brand offers it.

Take Airbnb as a prime example. When the company launched, the hotel industry was thriving. No one thought travelers would want to rent a stranger's apartment or home for the night. Yet, through exploration, Airbnb's founders discovered that travelers, especially younger generations, were craving more authentic, personal experiences. They didn't just want a bed for the night—they wanted to feel like they belonged in the place they were visiting. This desire wasn't being addressed by the hotel industry, which was focused on standardized luxury and efficiency.

By listening to these consumers and recognizing their need for a more local, intimate experience, Airbnb carved out an entirely new market. They didn't create the idea of short-term rentals, but they tapped into an underexplored aspect of travel—authenticity. Today, the company has completely reshaped the travel industry, becoming a global brand that stands for something more than just a place to stay.

Finding gaps in competitors' blind spots

Sometimes, the most valuable opportunities are sitting right in front of us, obscured by the success of our competitors. Exploration requires a keen eye for the weak spots in even the strongest brands. Competitor analysis is crucial here, not just to see what's working for others, but to identify what's missing.

Consider the rise of Dollar Shave Club. The men's grooming market was dominated by big names like Gillette and Schick, brands that had long controlled the razor industry with aggressive advertising and constant product innovations. The problem? These brands were locked into a pricing model that irritated customers. Razors were expensive, overly complex, and came with a lot of unnecessary bells and whistles.

Dollar Shave Club's exploration into customer dissatisfaction revealed an opportunity that the big brands were too focused on premium products to address. Instead of creating another high-end razor, they launched with a simple, affordable subscription model. The message was clear: shaving doesn't have to be complicated, and it certainly doesn't have to be expensive.

By focusing on what their competitors were ignoring—simplicity and affordability—Dollar Shave Club tapped into a market that was ripe for disruption. In a few short years, they captured millions of customers and completely redefined the men's grooming industry. Their success wasn't just about the product; it was about discovering an untapped market need that no one else was addressing.

Spotting emerging trends before they become mainstream

Sometimes, discovering untapped market potential is about recognizing a trend before it explodes. This takes foresight and a willingness to explore cultural or technological shifts that might seem small today but are poised for massive growth tomorrow. Brands that have their finger on the pulse of societal changes are often the ones that benefit most from these early signals.

Consider the growing demand for plant-based products. A decade ago, vegetarianism and veganism were considered niche markets, mostly catering to specific groups concerned with animal rights or environmental sustainability. But savvy brands began to notice that the conversation around plant-based eating was shifting. It wasn't just about ethics anymore—more consumers were becoming health-conscious, worried about the environmental impact of meat production, or simply curious about alternative diets.

Enter Beyond Meat. By spotting this cultural shift early and investing heavily in plant-based food technology, Beyond Meat positioned itself to ride the wave of a growing movement. They didn't wait for the trend to become mainstream—they became part of the reason it did. Today, the plant-based food market is one of the fastest-growing sectors in the food industry, with Beyond Meat leading the charge. Their exploration into the cultural and environmental zeitgeist paid off massively, allowing them to capitalize on a shift that others missed.

Unearthing opportunities in underserved markets

Sometimes, the greatest market potential lies in places no one is looking. Brands that focus too heavily on established consumer bases often overlook underserved or neglected markets. Exploration can reveal these opportunities, especially in regions or demographics that are ignored by larger competitors.

Take Toms Shoes, for example. Founder Blake Mycoskie saw an opportunity not just to sell shoes but to create a business model that catered to a different kind of consumer—one that cared deeply about social impact. His "One for One" model, where every pair of shoes sold resulted in a pair being donated to a child in need, spoke to a growing desire among consumers to make purchases that felt meaningful.

Toms didn't just find success in the shoe market; they tapped into an emotional need that wasn't being met by other brands. This model resonated deeply with socially conscious consumers who wanted their dollars to make a difference. By exploring the intersection of commerce and philanthropy, Toms was able to create a new type of brand loyalty—one rooted in purpose.

This strategy also helped them connect with markets that were otherwise underserved. In many developing countries, access to basic goods like shoes was limited. By turning their social mission into a central part of their brand, Toms not only sold shoes but built a movement that expanded their reach into markets where traditional shoe brands weren't even looking.

Exploration as an ongoing process

What all of these examples have in common is a commitment to exploration—not as a one-time activity, but as an ongoing process. Markets evolve, customer needs shift, and competitors come and go. Brands that continue to explore, that remain curious and open to what's next, are the ones that stay ahead.

Exploration doesn't have to be expensive or time-consuming, but it does require a mindset of constant curiosity. It's about asking "what if?" What if your product could solve a problem no one else is addressing? What if your brand could tap into an emerging trend before it becomes mainstream? What if you could serve a market that everyone else is ignoring?

By committing to exploration, brands open themselves up to discovering untapped potential that others might overlook. It's this willingness to dig deeper, to ask the hard questions, and to challenge assumptions that separates the brands that lead from those that follow.

CHAPTER 02
THE SECOND E

Essence

What is brand essence?
uncovering your brand's true DNA

At the heart of every great brand lies something intangible, something that transcends products, services, and even marketing. This is the brand's essence—its true DNA. Brand essence is the core idea that defines what the brand stands for, the emotional connection it creates, and the unique value it offers to its audience. It's not something that changes with trends or campaigns. Instead, it remains the constant that shapes how the brand is perceived and experienced across every touchpoint.

Think of a brand's essence as its soul. While a company's mission and vision might describe what it does and where it's headed, the essence explains who it is at its very core. It's the deeply ingrained values, beliefs, and personality traits that influence every decision the brand makes, from product development to customer service.

A strong brand essence provides clarity, focus, and direction. It's what makes consumers choose your brand over another, even if the products are similar. In an increasingly competitive market, where customers have more choices than ever, defining and articulating your brand essence is crucial to standing out and building lasting relationships.

The components of brand essence

Brand essence is often described as the single most important quality or idea that the brand represents, but it's built on several key components that work together to shape a brand's identity. These elements include emotional appeal, core values, brand promise, and personality.

Emotional appeal is the heart of brand essence. It's the feeling that a customer gets when they think of your brand or interact with it. Is your brand comforting? Exciting? Trustworthy? The emotional connection you create with your audience is often what keeps them loyal in the long term. For example, Apple's brand essence revolves around innovation and empowerment. It's not just about selling gadgets—it's about giving people the tools to think differently, to create, and to express themselves.

Core values underpin the brand's essence. They're the fundamental beliefs that guide everything the brand does. For Patagonia, environmental responsibility is at the core of its essence. It's not just a company that sells outdoor gear; it's a brand built around sustainability, making it clear that its values are non-negotiable.

Brand promise is closely linked to essence. It's what the brand consistently delivers to its customers, the expectation it sets. Nike, for instance, promises to inspire athletes at every level. Its essence, rooted in performance and empowerment, ensures that everything it does—from product design to marketing—lives up to that promise.

Personality is how the brand expresses itself. This could be through tone of voice, visual identity, or even customer service. A brand with a playful personality, like Ben & Jerry's, communicates its essence through quirky product names, humorous marketing, and a laid-back attitude. This personality helps consumers connect with the brand on a deeper level, making it feel human rather than corporate.

Why brand essence matters

In a world where competition is fierce, and products can be easily replicated, brand essence is the differentiator that creates lasting value. It's what makes your brand irreplaceable in the eyes of your customers. While competitors might copy your features or undercut your prices, they can't replicate the emotional bond that your brand essence creates.

Take Coca-Cola, for example. Its brand essence is all about happiness and togetherness. Every ad, every can of soda, and every interaction reflects this core message. Coca-Cola's success isn't just about selling soft drinks; it's about consistently delivering an emotional experience that transcends the product. This is why people remain loyal to the brand, even when there are countless other options.

Moreover, a clear brand essence provides consistency. In a time when consumers expect authenticity, brands that stay true to their essence are more likely to build trust. Consistency in tone, messaging, and experience shows customers that the brand knows who it is, which in turn helps them understand and connect with it. A brand that frequently changes its personality or messaging will confuse its audience and risk losing credibility.

How to uncover your brand's true DNA

Uncovering your brand's essence requires digging deeper than the surface-level features of your product or service. It's not about what you sell but why you sell it and how it makes people feel. Defining your brand essence begins with asking the right questions:

- What emotional connection do we want to build with our customers?

- What are the core values that drive everything we do?
- What promise are we making to our customers, and how do we deliver on it?
- What is the unique personality of our brand, and how does it express itself?

These questions force you to look beyond the functional aspects of your brand and think about the deeper meaning behind what you do. It's about identifying the core truth of your brand—the thing that, if removed, would fundamentally change what you stand for.

One approach to uncovering your brand essence is to look at the brand as a person. If your brand were a person, what would their personality be like? How would they speak? What values would they hold dear? This exercise can help distill complex ideas into a more relatable, human form.

It's also useful to listen to your customers. Often, they'll reveal the essence of your brand in ways you hadn't considered. What do your most loyal customers say about you? What adjectives do they use to describe your brand? These insights can provide valuable clues into what your brand truly represents to the people who matter most—your audience.

Staying true to your essence in a changing market

One of the challenges brands face is staying true to their essence while evolving with the market. Change is inevitable, and successful brands must adapt to shifting consumer needs, emerging technologies, and cultural trends. But how do you evolve without losing sight of your core identity?

The key is to maintain flexibility around your tactics while staying anchored in your brand's essence. Starbucks is a great example of a brand that has expanded and evolved without straying from its essence. Its essence revolves around being a "third place" between home and work—a space where people can relax, connect, and enjoy high-quality coffee. Over the years, Starbucks has added new product lines, embraced digital innovation, and entered new markets. But through it all, the brand has remained focused on creating that familiar and comforting coffeehouse experience.

On the other hand, brands that stray too far from their essence risk alienating their audience. Gap experienced this when it attempted to rebrand with a new logo in 2010. The sleek, modern design was a stark departure from its classic look, and the public backlash was swift. Customers felt that the new logo didn't represent Gap's essence, which was rooted in American casual style. The company quickly reverted to its original logo, realizing that it had lost sight of its core identity.

The essence of iconic brands

When we think of brands that have stood the test of time, it's often because they've maintained a strong and clear essence. Think about Harley-Davidson. Its essence is freedom and rebellion, and everything the brand does speaks to that. From the rumbling sound of the engines to the leather-clad riders, Harley-Davidson doesn't just sell motorcycles—it sells a lifestyle. The brand's essence is so deeply ingrained that it has cultivated a community of loyal customers who see themselves as part of something much bigger.

Similarly, Lego's brand essence is creativity and imagination. While the company has expanded into movies, video games, and theme parks, it has never strayed from this core essence. Everything Lego touches reinforces the idea that its products enable endless creative possibilities.

When a brand stays true to its essence, it builds a legacy. Customers come to trust the brand not just for the products it sells, but for what it stands for. And in today's world, where consumers are increasingly looking for brands that align with their values, this kind of authenticity is more valuable than ever.

Naming strategies: how to create a brand name that sticks

In the crowded world of brands, a name can be the difference between instant recognition and total obscurity. Your brand name is often the first impression you make on potential customers, so it needs to be memorable, meaningful, and aligned with your brand's essence. But creating a name that sticks isn't just about being catchy—it's about capturing the soul of your brand in a few simple words. A well-chosen name can convey your values, personality, and the promise your brand delivers.

Brand names like Google, Nike, and Tesla didn't become iconic by accident. Behind each of these names lies a story, a strategy that made them resonate with consumers. So how do you create a name that sticks in people's minds and feels like a natural extension of your brand's identity?

Naming isn't an afterthought—it's a strategic decision that can shape the way consumers perceive your brand for years to come. Here's how to craft a brand name that not only gets noticed but becomes a cornerstone of your brand's success.

What makes a brand name stick?

Before diving into strategies, it's important to understand what makes a name truly memorable. A sticky brand name has a few key characteristics:

- **Simplicity:** The best names are often the simplest. They're easy to spell, easy to say, and easy to remember. Brands like Apple or Zoom benefit from this simplicity, ensuring that their names don't get lost in translation or mispronounced.

- **Distinctiveness:** In a marketplace filled with competition, a brand name must stand out. If it blends in with the crowd, it's likely to be forgotten. Distinctive names like Google (an invented word) or Uber (with its sense of superiority) immediately capture attention because they don't sound like anything else.

- **Relevance:** While a name doesn't have to describe exactly what the brand does, it should be relevant to its industry or target audience. A good name evokes an idea, feeling, or image that aligns with the brand's purpose. Think of Dove, a brand name that evokes softness and purity—exactly what you'd want from a beauty product.

- **Emotional impact:** The best brand names don't just convey information—they trigger emotion. Whether it's excitement, curiosity, or trust, names that resonate on an emotional level are more likely to create lasting connections. Tesla, named after the inventor Nikola Tesla, evokes a sense of innovation and future-focused technology, making it more than just a car company.

- **Flexibility:** A great brand name should have the potential to grow with the brand. It needs to be adaptable enough to work across different markets, products, and platforms. Amazon started as an online bookstore, but its name—representing vastness and variety—allowed it to expand into nearly every retail category without losing its relevance.

Strategies for creating a memorable brand name

Crafting a brand name that ticks all these boxes is no easy task, but there are several strategies that can guide you toward the perfect choice.

1. Start with your brand's essence

The first step in naming is to go back to your brand's essence. Your brand essence is the DNA of your company, the thing that remains constant no matter how trends change. A good brand name should be a reflection of this essence.

For example, Nike's essence revolves around performance, competition, and victory. The name "Nike" comes from the Greek goddess of victory, perfectly aligning with the brand's focus on athletic achievement. When consumers hear the name, they immediately associate it with success and excellence.

Ask yourself: What does your brand stand for? What emotions do you want your customers to feel when they think of your brand? Your name should capture these qualities in a way that's simple and direct.

2. Play with language

Invented words can make for memorable brand names, especially when they are rooted in something meaningful. Google, for instance, comes from the mathematical term "googol," referring to an unfathomably large number. This ties in with the brand's mission of organizing an almost infinite amount of information on the web. Creating a new word allows your brand to stand out and avoids any baggage that comes with existing terms.

You can also look to other languages for inspiration. Brands like Häagen-Dazs used a foreign, exotic-sounding name to evoke luxury and quality, even though it wasn't based on any real words from Danish or Dutch. This linguistic playfulness can add a layer of mystery and sophistication to your brand.

Alternatively, combining two words or concepts can produce a name that's fresh and intriguing. Facebook is an example of this, combining "face" (social interaction) and "book" (a collection of information) to create something new and instantly recognizable.

3. Lean into storytelling

Every great brand has a story, and the name should be the opening line. Tesla, for example, not only nods to the famous inventor Nikola Tesla, but it also ties the brand to the innovative, forward-thinking spirit that he embodied. Similarly, brands like Virgin—

suggesting a fresh, untried approach—carry a narrative in their very name.

Consider how your brand name can be the starting point for a broader story. Can it hint at your brand's origins, its mission, or the problem it solves? Names like Slack (referring to reducing inefficiency in workplace communication) or Spotify (a combination of "spot" and "identify," representing the discovery of music) offer more than just a label—they offer a glimpse into the brand's purpose.

4. Use metaphors and symbols

Some of the best brand names work because they create strong mental images or metaphors. Amazon, for instance, immediately conjures the image of the world's largest river, symbolizing vastness, diversity, and flow—perfect for an e-commerce giant with a massive selection. Red Bull, on the other hand, uses the imagery of a bull to represent energy, power, and drive.

Metaphors help consumers create a mental association between the brand and the idea or feeling it represents. When brainstorming names, consider how you can use symbols, imagery, or metaphors to give your name more depth and meaning.

5. Ensure it's scalable and protectable

As much as creativity matters, there's also a practical side to naming. A brand name must be scalable, meaning it can grow with your brand as you expand into new categories or markets. You don't want to choose a name that's too specific to one product or region, as that could limit your potential.

Think about how your brand might evolve. If your name is too narrow, it could box you in. For example, if Netflix had chosen a name like "DVD-by-Mail" in its early days, it would have struggled to evolve into a streaming service. Instead, "Netflix" hints at flexibility and a broader focus on delivering entertainment through the internet, allowing the brand to grow without needing a rebrand.

Once you've landed on a name, the next step is to check its availability. Make sure it isn't already trademarked and that the domain name is available. Protecting your brand name legally ensures that you can grow without running into legal challenges down the road.

Finding the balance between creativity and clarity

One of the hardest parts of naming is finding the balance between creativity and clarity. While it's tempting to come up with something completely unique, don't sacrifice clarity in the process. If your name is too obscure, it might confuse customers instead of attracting them. The goal is to create a name that feels fresh but also gives consumers a sense of what you offer or how you make them feel.

When Uber launched, its name felt new and distinct, but it also hinted at superiority and convenience—traits that aligned with its essence of offering an elevated transportation experience. The name was both creative and clear, making it easy for consumers to understand and adopt.

Testing your name

Once you have a shortlist of potential names, it's crucial to test them. This can be as simple as running them by your target audience, conducting focus groups, or using social media polls to gauge reactions. The name needs to resonate with the people who matter most: your customers.

Make sure to test for things like pronunciation, memorability, and emotional response. How do people feel when they hear the name? Does it evoke the emotions or ideas you want it to? Are they likely to remember it after a single encounter?

Testing also helps identify potential pitfalls. A name that sounds perfect in one language might have unintended meanings in another, or it might be difficult to pronounce for certain audiences. A thorough test ensures that your name works across different regions, languages, and demographics.

A great name is the foundation of a great brand

Your brand name is more than just a label—it's a key part of your brand's identity. It sets the tone for how customers will experience your brand, making it essential to get it right. The process of naming might seem daunting, but with the right approach, it can be a rewarding journey that helps solidify your brand's place in the market.

When done well, a brand name can become an asset that drives recognition, loyalty, and emotional connection. It's not just about being catchy—it's about being meaningful, memorable, and unmistakably you.

Mission, vision, values: aligning your brand's essence with its goals

Every brand, whether large or small, is driven by purpose. At the center of this purpose are three core components: mission, vision, and values. These aren't just lofty ideas written on a corporate website—they are the foundational pillars that guide every decision a brand makes. Together, they shape a brand's identity, align its actions with its long-term goals, and help ensure consistency in both messaging and operations. When a brand successfully aligns its mission, vision, and values with its essence, it creates something powerful—a clear sense of direction that resonates with customers, employees, and stakeholders alike.

A brand's mission defines why it exists today. It's the practical, day-to-day explanation of what the brand does and who it serves. The mission should feel immediate and actionable, focusing on the brand's current purpose in the marketplace. Take TOMS, for example. Its mission is clear: "With every product you purchase, TOMS will help a person in need." The mission is not abstract; it's concrete and easily understood, telling customers exactly what the brand does and what to expect from every transaction. TOMS' mission also perfectly aligns with its essence—giving back. This straightforward yet powerful focus has helped the brand build loyalty, connecting with customers who care about social impact.

While the mission anchors a brand in the present, the vision is future-facing. It represents what the brand aspires to become. Think of it as a lighthouse, guiding the brand's long-term strategy and inspiring both employees and customers with the promise of a better future. A strong vision helps ensure that every decision the brand makes today is aligned with its long-term goals. For example, Patagonia's vision isn't just to sell outdoor gear; it's to "use business to inspire and implement solutions to the environmental crisis." This bold, ambitious vision positions Patagonia not only as an outdoor brand but as a leader in environmental advocacy, giving it a clear sense of purpose beyond profit. The brand's commitment to sustainability, recycling initiatives, and activism all reflect this vision, creating a bond with eco-conscious consumers who share the same goals.

But a brand's essence can't simply live in the now or in the future—it needs values to act as the moral compass that keeps everything in check. Values are the deeply held beliefs that inform how the brand operates, communicates, and interacts with the world. They influence the way a brand responds to challenges, how it treats its customers and employees, and what it stands for in the face of adversity. Values are what keep a brand authentic. For example, Ben & Jerry's has a clear set of values centered on social justice, equality, and sustainability. These values shine through not only in the brand's product sourcing and business practices but in its outspoken stance on issues like climate change and racial justice. The brand doesn't just talk about its values; it actively lives them, ensuring that its actions align with its deeply held beliefs.

When mission, vision, and values are fully aligned with a brand's essence, they serve as a guide for every action the brand takes, ensuring consistency and authenticity across all touchpoints. But this alignment doesn't happen by accident. Brands need to continuously assess whether their day-to-day operations are truly reflecting their mission. If there's a disconnect—say, a brand that claims to prioritize customer service but consistently fails to respond to customer feedback—the result is a loss of trust and credibility.

A brand that successfully aligns its mission, vision, and values with its essence is Apple. Its mission, "to bring the best user experience to customers through innovative hardware, software, and services," is clear and actionable. Everything Apple creates, from its intuitive product design to its seamless ecosystem, reflects this mission. But Apple's vision goes beyond creating beautiful products; it aims to "leave the world better than we found it." This focus on innovation with a purpose drives Apple's long-term strategy, from its investment in renewable energy to its commitment to reducing carbon emissions. Apple's values—simplicity, privacy, and accessibility—are reflected in everything from its minimalist packaging to its commitment to user privacy. These values are non-negotiable and remain central to Apple's brand identity, helping it build an emotional connection with customers who appreciate the brand's focus on both innovation and integrity.

However, aligning mission, vision, and values isn't always smooth sailing. Brands can lose their way, especially when they prioritize short-term gains over long-term goals. Take Uber, which experienced rapid growth and market dominance but faced criticism for its internal culture and ethical practices. While Uber's mission was clear—making transportation as reliable as running water—its values around transparency, respect, and fairness came under scrutiny. The disconnect between the brand's operations and its values led to public backlash, forcing Uber to reevaluate its culture and leadership. This misalignment cost the brand more than just reputation—it eroded customer trust, proving that a strong mission alone is not enough. A brand must live its values and remain true to its vision, even during periods of rapid growth or external pressure.

Successful brands understand that mission, vision, and values are not static concepts. They need to evolve with the brand, ensuring that they remain relevant and aligned with both internal and external realities. But while missions can evolve and visions may shift, values are less flexible. They are the foundation of the brand's essence and should remain steady, no matter how the market or business environment changes. A strong set of values acts as an anchor, allowing the brand to weather storms without losing sight of who it is.

Aligning mission, vision, and values isn't just about creating a brand strategy—it's about creating a meaningful and authentic brand experience. When these three elements are in sync, they act as a powerful force, guiding the brand toward its goals while building deep connections with its audience. Customers today are more discerning than ever, seeking out brands that don't just deliver great products or services but that also stand for something. They want to know what your brand believes in, what it's working toward, and how it behaves when no one is watching.

In essence, mission, vision, and values are the soul of the brand's essence, connecting the brand's DNA to its long-term aspirations. When brands take the time to define these elements clearly—and more importantly, live by them—they create not just a business but a brand with purpose. That purpose becomes the driving force behind customer loyalty, employee engagement, and long-term growth.

Personality and tone of voice: crafting a persona customers trust

Behind every successful brand is a distinct personality. Just like people, brands have attitudes, values, and quirks that make them memorable. This personality isn't just about flashy logos or clever taglines—it's about how the brand expresses itself across every interaction, from marketing campaigns to customer service. And at the heart of this brand personality is its tone of voice. The way a brand speaks plays a crucial role in shaping how it is perceived, how it connects with customers, and ultimately, how it builds trust.

Brand personality and tone of voice aren't just abstract concepts. They are the tools that give a brand its humanity, making it relatable and distinct in a sea of competitors. A well-crafted brand personality creates an emotional connection, while a consistent tone of voice ensures that connection remains strong and recognizable no matter how or where customers engage with the brand.

Why personality matters

In an increasingly saturated market, products and services alone are often not enough to stand out. Consumers are bombarded with choices, and in many cases, several brands offer similar solutions. What sets a brand apart isn't always its product—it's the way the brand makes people feel. Personality plays a huge role in this. A brand with a clearly defined personality becomes more than just a provider of goods or services; it becomes something customers can relate to and feel connected to.

Take Nike, for example. Nike's brand personality is strong, bold, and motivational. It's not just selling shoes—it's selling a lifestyle of performance, ambition, and success. Every piece of communication, whether it's a commercial or a social media post, reflects this personality. Nike isn't just another athletic brand; it's a cheerleader for anyone striving to be their best self. That's why its iconic "Just Do It" slogan resonates so deeply—it's a message that speaks directly to the mindset of athletes and goal-driven individuals.

A clear brand personality also provides consistency. Customers know what to expect when they interact with the brand. Whether it's funny, serious, friendly, or professional, a consistent personality reassures customers that they can trust the brand. It feels familiar, reliable, and true to itself. Inconsistency, on the other hand, can be jarring. A brand that's serious one moment and flippant the next risks confusing or alienating its audience.

Developing your brand's tone of voice

If personality is the core of who a brand is, then tone of voice is how that personality speaks. It's the distinct way a brand communicates with its audience across all touchpoints—whether it's a social media post, an email, or even the copy on its website. Tone of voice plays a vital role in building trust, because how you say something can be just as important as what you say.

Tone of voice should be shaped by the brand's personality and aligned with its audience. A playful, witty tone might work perfectly for a brand like Wendy's, which has made a name for itself with its snarky, humorous social media presence. But that same tone wouldn't work for a brand like Volvo, which relies on a tone that conveys safety, reliability, and professionalism. Both brands are successful because their tones align with the expectations and emotions of their target audiences.

One brand that has mastered tone of voice is Mailchimp. As a B2B company offering email marketing services, Mailchimp could easily default to a dry, corporate tone. But instead, it opts for a friendly, approachable voice that reflects its playful personality. Its language is simple and conversational, helping small businesses feel confident rather than overwhelmed by the task of email marketing. By humanizing its brand, Mailchimp not only makes its product more accessible but also builds trust through an approachable, user-friendly persona.

Consistency is key when it comes to tone of voice. A brand that jumps between formal and casual or technical and conversational will confuse its audience. It's essential to develop guidelines that ensure every piece of communication reflects the same tone. This doesn't mean being robotic—flexibility is important to adapt to different contexts—but the overall tone should always reflect the brand's core personality.

Building trust through authenticity

Trust is one of the most valuable currencies a brand can have. In today's world, consumers are increasingly skeptical of brands that feel inauthentic or opportunistic. This is where personality and tone of voice become critical. Brands that can craft a genuine personality and stick to it build stronger, more lasting connections with their audience.

Authenticity comes from being true to your brand's values and mission. Consumers are quick to spot when a brand is faking it. If a brand tries to jump on a trending cause that doesn't align with its core values, or suddenly shifts tone to capitalize on a moment, it risks damaging trust. Think of Pepsi's infamous ad campaign featuring Kendall Jenner, which attempted to leverage social justice movements but came across as tone-deaf and opportunistic. The brand faced backlash because the message and tone felt disconnected from its true essence.

In contrast, Patagonia's tone of voice is a perfect reflection of its brand essence. The company's commitment to environmental activism is woven into every part of its communication. Whether it's a social media post, a product description, or a public statement, Patagonia speaks with a tone of urgency, care, and respect for the environment. This consistency reinforces the brand's authenticity, making it clear that Patagonia's actions and words are aligned.

When customers see that a brand's tone of voice is consistent with its values and mission, they are more likely to trust it. And trust, once earned, translates into loyalty, advocacy, and long-term relationships.

Creating an emotional connection

A brand's tone of voice also plays a key role in creating emotional connections. The words a brand uses and the way it communicates can evoke feelings of joy, excitement, trust, or even nostalgia. This emotional connection is what turns a one-time customer into a loyal brand advocate.

Consider brands like Disney, which has a tone of voice that evokes wonder, magic, and nostalgia. Disney isn't just selling movies, theme parks, or merchandise—it's selling an experience, a return to childhood, and a sense of possibility. The tone is always upbeat, filled with imagination, and designed to inspire happiness. This emotional tone is critical to how customers experience the brand, and it has helped Disney build one of the most loyal followings in the world.

On the other end of the spectrum, Dove's tone of voice is gentle, inclusive, and empowering. Through campaigns like "Real Beauty," Dove speaks directly to women in a way that uplifts and reassures. Its tone reflects its commitment to body positivity and self-esteem, creating a strong emotional bond with customers who value authenticity and kindness. Dove isn't just selling soap—it's selling confidence and self-love, and its tone is critical to delivering that message.

Bringing personality to life across channels

A well-crafted brand personality doesn't just exist in ads or marketing materials—it's present across every channel and touchpoint where the brand interacts with its audience. From social media to customer service, packaging to product descriptions, every interaction is an opportunity to reinforce the brand's personality and tone of voice.

A great example is Netflix, which has mastered the art of infusing its playful and clever tone across platforms. Whether it's through witty tweets or quirky show descriptions, Netflix's personality shines through, making it not just a streaming service but a source of entertainment in its own right. This consistency across channels makes the brand feel familiar and approachable, helping it build a strong rapport with its audience.

At the same time, tone of voice can extend to customer service interactions. Brands like Zappos have built their reputation on providing exceptional service with a tone of genuine care and friendliness. Every interaction with a customer is seen as an opportunity to reinforce the brand's personality and create a positive emotional experience. This attention to tone has earned Zappos a reputation for not just selling shoes but for caring deeply about its customers.

Personality and tone as the foundation of trust

At its core, a brand's personality and tone of voice are what make it feel human. They provide the bridge between the brand's essence and how it communicates with the world. Crafting a persona that feels authentic and consistent is key to building trust with customers, especially in a market where consumers are more discerning than ever.

A brand that knows who it is—and expresses that consistently—becomes more than just a business. It becomes something people can relate to, engage with, and trust. And when customers trust a brand, they are not only more likely to buy from it but to advocate for it, creating a relationship that goes far beyond transactions.

Brand elasticity: how far can your brand stretch?

A brand is like a rubber band—strong and flexible, but with limits. Push it too far, and it might snap; stretch it just right, and it can expand into new categories, markets, or even entirely different industries. This is the idea behind brand elasticity: the ability of a brand to extend beyond its original product or service offering without losing its identity or credibility. For companies looking to grow, brand elasticity offers a path to innovation and diversification. But knowing how far your brand can stretch—and when to stop—is key to ensuring long-term success.

Brand elasticity isn't just about launching a new product or tapping into a new audience. It's about expanding in ways that feel natural, organic, and aligned with the brand's core values. Some brands can stretch remarkably far—think Apple, which began as a computer company and has since become synonymous with everything from smartphones to wearables and entertainment. Others, however, struggle to maintain credibility when they stray too far from their essence, like Harley-Davidson's ill-fated attempt to launch a line of perfume in the 1990s.

So, how do you determine your brand's limits and avoid overextension? Let's explore the nuances of brand elasticity and how you can stretch your brand without breaking it.

The core of brand elasticity: staying true to your essence

The first rule of brand elasticity is to stay true to your brand's essence. A successful brand extension builds on what already makes the brand strong, enhancing its identity rather than confusing it. At the core of elasticity is the idea that your brand stands for something deeper than the specific products it sells. If your brand is built around a strong value or concept, like innovation or sustainability, that essence can carry over into new areas.

Take Nike, for instance. The brand began by selling athletic shoes but has expanded into apparel, accessories, and even digital fitness solutions. What allows Nike to stretch so successfully is its core essence of performance and empowerment. No matter what product it launches, Nike's focus on helping athletes achieve their best is clear. The brand can introduce running gear, fitness apps, or even sports-related technology, and it all feels consistent with the brand's core identity.

But the stretch only works if it aligns with the brand's mission and audience expectations. If Nike suddenly decided to launch kitchen appliances, it would be an awkward fit because it doesn't resonate with the brand's purpose. Even a globally trusted brand has boundaries, and recognizing where those boundaries lie is crucial to maintaining brand integrity.

Extending into new categories: the art of logical expansion

One of the most common ways brands stretch is by moving into adjacent product categories. This type of extension is often the easiest to pull off because it feels like a natural evolution of the brand.

A logical extension builds on the brand's existing strengths and creates new opportunities without confusing or alienating its audience.

Apple is a prime example of brand elasticity done right. Originally a computer company, Apple ventured into the music industry with the iPod, then expanded further into mobile technology with the iPhone. Each of these moves felt like a natural progression, anchored in Apple's essence of innovation, simplicity, and high-quality design. The company's ability to stretch its brand into different tech products worked because it stayed true to its roots—making complex technology accessible and beautifully designed.

The key to a successful stretch into a new category is to ensure the extension feels intuitive to the customer. Starbucks, for example, successfully expanded its brand beyond coffee into snacks, beverages, and even home products like coffee makers. These extensions make sense to the customer because they align with the Starbucks experience—comfort, quality, and an elevated sense of indulgence.

However, when a brand stretches into a category that doesn't feel connected to its essence, it can create dissonance. Colgate's attempt to launch a line of frozen meals is one of the classic examples of brand elasticity gone wrong. Colgate's essence is tied to oral hygiene, and customers found the idea of Colgate-branded food unappetizing. The brand's stretch didn't make sense, and it ultimately damaged the credibility of both the new product and the core brand.

Entering new markets: leveraging trust and recognition

Another way brands can stretch is by entering new geographic markets. Global expansion offers the chance to introduce a brand to entirely new audiences, but it also requires careful navigation of cultural differences and local expectations. While the brand's essence should remain consistent, the execution may need to be adapted for different markets.

Take McDonald's as a case study. The fast-food giant has successfully expanded into nearly every corner of the world by maintaining its core essence—convenient, affordable fast food—while adapting its menu and messaging to local tastes. In India, for instance, McDonald's offers vegetarian options and removes beef from its menu to align with cultural preferences. This balance between staying true to its essence and being flexible enough to adapt to local markets has allowed McDonald's to become a global powerhouse without losing its identity.

However, not every brand can stretch globally with ease. When Walmart expanded into Germany in the late 1990s, it faced a cultural clash. German shoppers were turned off by Walmart's "greeters" and felt the American-style customer service was intrusive. Walmart's failure to adapt its brand to the local market led to a significant loss of trust, and the company eventually had to withdraw. The lesson here is clear: brand elasticity across markets requires both consistency in the core message and sensitivity to local nuances.

Diversification vs. dilution: knowing when to stop

There's a fine line between diversification and dilution. Brands that stretch too far beyond their core identity risk confusing customers and losing the trust they've built. A brand that tries to be everything to everyone often ends up being nothing to anyone.

Harley-Davidson's infamous attempt to launch a perfume line is a textbook example of brand dilution. Harley's essence is rooted in freedom, rebellion, and the open road—qualities that are deeply connected to its motorcycles. Perfume, on the other hand, felt completely disconnected from this identity. The brand's foray into fragrance left customers confused and damaged its credibility. The failure of the perfume line was a clear indication that Harley had stretched too far, into a category that didn't resonate with its core values.

Brand elasticity only works when it feels like a logical extension of the brand's existing strengths. Stretching too far risks not just a failed product but also the weakening of the core brand. This is why many luxury brands, like Rolex or Hermès, are so careful about how they expand. They prioritize protecting their core identity and maintaining exclusivity, rather than chasing every new opportunity that arises.

The power of emotional elasticity

Brand elasticity isn't just about products and markets—it's also about the emotional range a brand can cover. Some brands are highly elastic when it comes to emotional tone, able to shift between different moods and feelings without losing their identity. Coca-Cola, for instance, stretches between nostalgia, joy, and togetherness in its marketing, all while maintaining a consistent brand essence centered on happiness and refreshment. Whether it's a classic ad from the 1970s or a modern digital campaign, Coca-Cola's emotional elasticity allows it to stay relevant across generations and cultures.

The power of emotional elasticity is that it allows brands to engage with customers on multiple levels, creating deeper connections. However, this kind of stretch still requires consistency. A brand can explore different emotional tones, but the underlying message must always reflect the brand's core essence. If a brand's emotional messaging becomes inconsistent, it risks confusing the audience and weakening its overall identity.

Stretching into the future: innovation and adaptation

As industries evolve and consumer needs change, brand elasticity becomes increasingly important for long-term success. Innovation is at the heart of elasticity, but it must be balanced with staying true to what makes the brand unique. Brands like Amazon, which began as an online bookstore and expanded into nearly every retail category imaginable, showcase how innovation paired with a clear sense of identity can drive exponential growth.

The future of brand elasticity will likely involve even more cross-industry collaborations, digital transformations, and unexpected extensions. But for brands to successfully navigate this future, they must remember that elasticity is about alignment. It's not about how far you can stretch—it's about how far you can stretch while still staying true to who you are.

A brand that redefined its essence to pivot in the market

When a brand faces market shifts, consumer behavior changes, or internal challenges, it sometimes needs to make a drastic move: redefine its essence. For many companies, staying true to their core identity while adapting to new realities is key to survival. But for others, evolving or completely reimagining their essence is what allows them to remain relevant and competitive. One of the most well-known examples of this strategic shift is Netflix—a brand that successfully redefined its essence to pivot from a DVD rental service to a global entertainment powerhouse.

In its early days, Netflix had a clear, practical mission: to provide an easier and more convenient way to rent DVDs by mailing them directly to customers. At its core, Netflix's essence was about access—making entertainment more available to the average consumer without the late fees and hassle of traditional rental stores like Blockbuster. Netflix's red envelopes became iconic, and the company found early success by sticking to this simple, efficient model.

However, by the late 2000s, the rise of digital streaming, paired with the inevitable decline of physical media, signaled that Netflix's initial essence might not be sustainable in the long term. The DVD rental market was shrinking, and consumer preferences were rapidly shifting toward instant, on-demand streaming. Netflix could have clung to its DVD rental model, but the company recognized that the entertainment landscape was evolving, and they needed to evolve with it. So, Netflix redefined its essence, shifting from "DVD rental by mail" to "streaming entertainment for all." This pivot not only reoriented the company's business model but also transformed its identity.

What made Netflix's pivot particularly successful was its ability to stay rooted in one key aspect of its original essence: access to entertainment. The shift to streaming wasn't a total departure from what Netflix stood for. It simply took the core value of access and modernized it for a digital age, making the transition feel seamless for its customers. By focusing on what they had always promised —convenience, affordability, and entertainment—Netflix managed to retain its loyal customer base while attracting millions of new users.

The pivot didn't stop there. Netflix pushed its redefined essence even further by entering the world of content creation. Instead of merely offering access to films and TV shows produced by other studios, Netflix began producing its own original content, launching Netflix Originals in 2013 with the hit series *House of Cards*. This move shifted Netflix's essence once again, from being a content distributor to a content creator. Now, Netflix wasn't just offering access to entertainment—it was shaping the future of entertainment.

This second pivot represented a more significant evolution in Netflix's brand essence. The company was no longer just about convenience and access; it was about innovation and leadership in the entertainment industry. Netflix's investment in original programming signaled a commitment to becoming a tastemaker, a brand that could not only distribute but also create the most talked-about content. The essence of Netflix had evolved from a practical service to a creative force that defines cultural moments, from *Stranger Things* to *The Crown*.

What's remarkable about Netflix's evolution is how it managed to remain consistent in its core promise—bringing entertainment to people—while constantly pushing the boundaries of what that meant. The brand's ability to redefine its essence without losing sight of its foundational values is a lesson for any company facing a rapidly changing market. Netflix didn't wait until it was forced to change; it proactively embraced innovation, which allowed it to stay ahead of competitors and reshape the industry on its terms.

There are risks involved in redefining a brand's essence. When done poorly, it can confuse customers or dilute the brand's identity. For example, in the early 2010s, Gap attempted to modernize its logo, shifting away from its iconic blue box in favor of a minimalist design. The backlash was swift, with customers feeling that the new logo didn't reflect Gap's essence as a classic, American fashion brand. Within a week, Gap reverted to its original logo. The lesson? A brand's essence is deeply ingrained in how customers perceive it, and any changes need to feel authentic and aligned with the brand's core identity.

Netflix, however, navigated its pivot by ensuring that each evolution was a natural extension of its original mission. The company's willingness to take calculated risks, embrace new technologies, and enter uncharted territories allowed it to continuously redefine what it meant to be an entertainment brand. Today, Netflix is not just a platform where people watch content; it's a cultural institution that shapes global entertainment trends and delivers original, award-winning programming.

The key takeaway from Netflix's journey is that a brand's essence doesn't have to be rigid. While core values should remain consistent, the expression of those values can and should evolve to meet changing market demands. Brands that are willing to redefine themselves, without abandoning what makes them special, are the ones most likely to thrive in the long run. Netflix's story serves as a masterclass in how to pivot, stretch, and grow without losing sight of what makes your brand uniquely valuable.

CHAPTER 03
THE THIRD E

Expression

The power of storytelling: building emotional connections

Humans have been telling stories for thousands of years. It's how we've passed down knowledge, traditions, and values. Stories connect us on an emotional level in ways that facts and data simply cannot. In branding, storytelling is a tool that can transform a faceless company into something personal, relatable, and memorable. While products or services may catch attention, it's a brand's story that truly sticks. A great story doesn't just sell—it creates a lasting emotional connection between the brand and its audience.

At its core, brand storytelling is about more than just marketing. It's about creating a narrative that reflects the brand's values, mission, and essence. When done right, storytelling gives the brand a voice and personality, turning customers into loyal advocates. It's the difference between being just another name on the shelf and being a brand people love and trust.

Take Nike, for example. Nike doesn't just sell sneakers or athletic gear—it sells the idea of overcoming challenges and pushing boundaries. Its storytelling, through powerful campaigns like *Just Do It*, taps into universal themes of resilience, strength, and the pursuit of greatness. Whether it's telling the story of a young athlete overcoming obstacles or showing how a simple pair of shoes can empower someone, Nike's storytelling creates a deep emotional bond with its audience. This bond has turned Nike into a brand that transcends its products, becoming a symbol of inspiration and self-belief.

Why storytelling works: the emotional connection

The real power of storytelling lies in its ability to evoke emotion. People make decisions based on how they feel, not just what they know. A well-crafted story can inspire, motivate, or even bring out nostalgia. When a brand taps into these emotions, it connects with its audience in a meaningful way. It's not just about what the brand offers, but what it represents.

Consider Apple. Its storytelling often revolves around innovation, creativity, and empowerment. From its iconic *Think Different* campaign to its product launch presentations, Apple weaves a narrative that speaks to the creative potential within everyone. The emotional connection Apple has built with its customers is so strong that many see their iPhone or MacBook as an extension of themselves, rather than just a piece of technology. This emotional loyalty is what allows Apple to maintain its position as a leader in the tech industry, even when competitors offer similar products.

Stories allow brands to go beyond transactional relationships with their customers. Instead of focusing solely on selling, they can focus on building a relationship that feels personal. Storytelling allows customers to see themselves in the brand's journey, creating a shared experience that resonates deeply.

The structure of a compelling brand story

While every brand's story is unique, the structure of a compelling narrative is often the same. It usually follows a classic arc: the introduction of a challenge or problem, the journey to overcome it, and a resolution that delivers value or insight. This structure mirrors the stories we've been telling for centuries, from ancient myths to modern-day films, and it's incredibly effective in capturing and holding attention.

Patagonia, the outdoor clothing brand, tells stories that follow this exact arc. Its brand stories often revolve around environmental challenges and the efforts to overcome them, whether it's a documentary about preserving wilderness or highlighting its initiative to repair old gear rather than sell new products. The "problem" is clear: environmental degradation. The journey is Patagonia's commitment to sustainability and its call for customers to be part of the solution. The resolution? A message of hope, showing that together, we can make a difference. Patagonia's storytelling not only aligns with its brand essence but also invites customers to join a cause larger than themselves.

The power of this structure lies in its ability to take audiences on a journey. People are naturally drawn to narratives that have a sense of progression, transformation, and a satisfying resolution. This is why brand stories that follow this arc tend to leave a lasting impression. They don't just present a product—they present a journey that consumers want to be part of.

Authenticity in brand storytelling

One of the most important aspects of storytelling in branding is authenticity. Consumers are smarter and more skeptical than ever, and they can easily spot a story that feels forced or inauthentic. To build trust, brands must ensure their stories reflect their true values and mission. When a brand's story aligns with its actions and identity, it becomes credible. When there's a disconnect, it can feel manipulative, leading to loss of trust.

A good example of authentic storytelling comes from Dove. Its *Real Beauty* campaign has been running for over a decade and focuses on challenging narrow beauty standards. Dove's story is about celebrating real women with real bodies, and the brand consistently shows this across its marketing. The campaign resonates because it aligns with Dove's essence of inclusivity and empowerment. Rather than using airbrushed models, Dove highlights everyday women, sending a powerful message that beauty isn't one-size-fits-all. This authenticity has helped Dove build deep emotional connections with its audience, many of whom feel seen and valued by the brand's messaging.

On the flip side, brands that use storytelling simply as a marketing tactic, without any real connection to their values, risk alienating their audience. When Pepsi launched its infamous protest-themed commercial with Kendall Jenner, it tried to tap into the global movement for social justice. However, the ad backfired because it was perceived as inauthentic—a superficial attempt to capitalize on serious issues. The lesson here is clear: storytelling must be rooted in truth. Consumers don't just want a good story; they want a story that reflects the brand's values and actions.

Using customer stories to amplify the brand

While brands often focus on telling their own stories, some of the most powerful narratives come from customers themselves. Real customer stories add a layer of authenticity that no marketing campaign can replicate. By showcasing real experiences, brands can demonstrate their impact in the lives of their customers, building trust and credibility in the process.

Glossier, the beauty brand, is an excellent example of this approach. From its earliest days, Glossier has encouraged customers to share their own beauty routines, struggles, and transformations. Rather than simply talking about their products, Glossier lets its community tell the story. Customers feel like they are part of the brand, and their stories create a ripple effect, attracting more people who relate to those experiences. By giving customers a platform, Glossier has built a loyal following that feels personally invested in the brand's journey.

Incorporating customer stories into a brand's narrative also allows the brand to expand its reach. These stories resonate more because they feel real, relatable, and accessible. Consumers are far more likely to trust the experiences of their peers than the claims of a corporation. When brands encourage their customers to share their stories, they tap into a powerful form of word-of-mouth marketing that is both authentic and engaging.

Evolving your story

As markets change and brands evolve, storytelling should also evolve. A brand's story isn't static—it should grow as the brand expands into new territories or introduces new products. However, the core message should remain consistent, reflecting the brand's essence.

Netflix is a great example of a brand that has adapted its story over time. Initially, Netflix was simply a DVD rental service, but as streaming technology became more prevalent, Netflix's story shifted. Now, it isn't just about delivering content—it's about creating it. Netflix has become synonymous with groundbreaking original programming, and its story now revolves around innovation, creativity, and changing the way the world consumes entertainment. The brand's story has evolved, but the focus on making entertainment accessible to all has remained constant.

Brands that can evolve their story while staying true to their core values tend to build stronger, more resilient connections with their audience. People love a good narrative arc—watching a brand grow, adapt, and overcome challenges can deepen loyalty and engagement. The key is to ensure that, no matter how the story changes, it always reflects the brand's fundamental mission and values.

From storytelling to storyselling: turning narratives into conversions

Storytelling has always been a powerful tool for creating emotional connections with audiences, but in the world of branding, it's not just about telling a great story. It's about turning that story into sales — moving from storytelling to **storyselling**. A brand's narrative can do more than just engage; it can motivate action, drive conversions, and build customer loyalty. When brands combine a compelling story with clear, actionable elements, they transform passive audiences into active buyers.

Storyselling isn't a new concept, but with consumers today craving authenticity and emotional resonance, its importance has never been greater. Brands that master the art of storyselling are able to weave their product or service into a larger narrative that not only connects emotionally but also inspires people to take the next step, whether that's making a purchase, signing up for a service, or sharing the brand's message with others.

Storyselling: creating urgency through narrative

One of the key differences between storytelling and storyselling is the presence of a clear call to action. While storytelling might entertain or inform, storyselling is about encouraging your audience to make a decision. The most successful storyselling strategies blend an emotional connection with a sense of urgency or necessity, positioning the product as the natural solution to a problem.

Take the brand Warby Parker, for example. Warby Parker's story isn't just about selling eyewear; it's about solving a problem that many consumers face: the high cost of glasses. The company's story positions itself as a disruptor of the traditional eyewear industry, offering stylish, affordable glasses without the retail markup. By weaving this narrative into its marketing, Warby Parker turns its origin story into a selling point. The brand's "buy a pair, give a pair" model taps into customers' desire for social responsibility, creating an emotional connection that's directly linked to the purchase decision.

The story of Warby Parker isn't just entertaining—it's designed to drive action. The narrative around affordability and social impact creates a sense of urgency, making customers feel like they're not just buying glasses but supporting a movement. This combination of storytelling and actionable messaging has helped Warby Parker become a favorite among millennial consumers who want their purchases to have purpose.

Building desire through emotional triggers

Storyselling works best when it taps into core human emotions like fear, joy, hope, or desire. By understanding what motivates your audience, you can craft a story that resonates with their needs and aspirations, making your product or service the obvious solution. It's not about manipulation; it's about presenting a story that speaks to their challenges and goals in a meaningful way.

Apple is a master at this. Think about any Apple product launch—each one is a carefully orchestrated event that blends storytelling and product features to create desire. Apple doesn't just tell you what the new iPhone can do; it paints a picture of how it will improve your life. Through emotionally charged visuals and aspirational language, Apple makes the audience believe that owning the latest iPhone will make them more creative, productive, and connected. It's not just about the product's specs; it's about the lifestyle it enables.

This emotional trigger is what moves Apple's customers from passive viewers of its marketing to eager buyers, often willing to queue for hours to get their hands on the latest release. The story Apple tells through its advertising and product launches creates a deep desire not just for the product itself but for the experience that comes with it.

Storyselling as a trust-building tool

Trust is the foundation of any successful sales process, and stories are one of the best ways to build that trust. A brand's story can establish credibility, demonstrate expertise, and show authenticity—all of which are critical for convincing potential customers to take action. Storyselling allows brands to subtly highlight their strengths while reinforcing why customers should trust them.

Dollar Shave Club leveraged storyselling perfectly with its now-famous launch video. In less than two minutes, the brand told a compelling story about why expensive razors are unnecessary, while positioning its subscription model as the smart, no-nonsense alternative. The video, which used humor and honesty, quickly went viral, establishing Dollar Shave Club as a trusted disruptor in the razor industry. It didn't just entertain; it sold the concept of affordable razors, delivered straight to your door. The humor in the story made the brand relatable, while the simplicity of the offer made the buying decision easy.

By telling a story that resonated with the frustrations of its audience, Dollar Shave Club built immediate trust. The blend of humor, relatability, and a clear value proposition resulted in high conversion rates and laid the foundation for the brand's explosive growth.

Creating a seamless transition from story to sale

Storyselling works best when the transition from narrative to action feels natural. If the story is compelling but the product feels disconnected, the audience may lose interest. However, when the product is an integral part of the story, it becomes a logical and desirable next step.

Consider Tom's Shoes, a brand that has built its entire business model on storyselling. Tom's *One for One* promise—where every pair of shoes purchased leads to a pair being donated to someone in need—isn't just part of their story; it is their story. The emotional weight of this promise creates a direct link between the story and the purchase decision. Customers aren't just buying shoes; they're participating in a movement that aligns with their values. The story isn't complete without their action, which is why Tom's has seen such success in driving conversions.

By seamlessly integrating the product into the story, brands like Tom's make it easier for customers to connect emotionally while feeling good about their purchase decision. The key is to make the product an essential part of the narrative—something that enhances the story's resolution and gives the customer a reason to act.

User-generated stories: amplifying storyselling

One of the most powerful ways to amplify storyselling is through user-generated content. When customers share their own stories about how they use your product or service, it adds a layer of authenticity and trust that no brand-crafted narrative can match. These real-life stories turn customers into advocates and help drive conversions by showing others how your product fits into their lives.

Brands like Glossier have mastered this approach, encouraging customers to share their beauty routines and product experiences on social media. These user stories create a continuous loop of storyselling, where customers tell their own stories and, in turn, influence others to join the brand's community. Glossier's strength lies in its ability to make every customer feel like part of the story, seamlessly blending their experiences with the brand's larger narrative.

User-generated stories can also act as powerful social proof, showing potential customers that people just like them have had positive experiences with the brand. This layer of peer endorsement adds credibility and makes the decision to buy feel safer and more informed.

Measuring the impact of storyselling

For all its emotional power, storyselling ultimately needs to drive measurable results. Brands need to track how well their stories are converting viewers into customers and fine-tune their narratives to optimize performance. Metrics like engagement rates, click-through rates, and conversion rates can offer valuable insights into which stories resonate most and which fall flat.

Many brands use A/B testing to experiment with different story formats, calls to action, or emotional triggers. This allows them to refine their storyselling approach, ensuring that each element—from the narrative arc to the product pitch—works seamlessly to move the audience toward a purchase decision.

For example, Patagonia's environmental storytelling often incorporates calls to action that encourage customers to not only buy products but also support environmental causes. Patagonia tracks engagement through social media, website clicks, and sales to measure how effectively these stories are driving both sales and activism. The brand constantly evolves its storyselling approach to ensure it aligns with both its mission and its business goals.

Visual identity: building a brand's visual language

In today's crowded marketplace, where customers are constantly bombarded with messages, a brand's visual identity acts as its first impression. It's the visual shorthand that communicates who the brand is and what it stands for before a single word is spoken. A strong visual identity isn't just about looking good—it's about conveying the brand's essence and values in a way that resonates with its audience. From logos to color schemes, typography to packaging, every visual element tells a story. When these elements are thoughtfully aligned, they create a cohesive visual language that not only grabs attention but fosters recognition and loyalty.

A brand's visual identity should do more than just attract eyeballs. It needs to reflect the brand's personality, communicate its values, and create an emotional connection. Think of it as the visual translation of a brand's DNA, where every design choice serves a purpose.

The power of the logo

At the heart of any visual identity is the logo. This single graphic becomes the face of the brand and is often the most recognizable element. Logos act as symbols, instantly recalling emotions, experiences, and expectations tied to the brand. A great logo distills a brand's essence into a simple, memorable image that stands out in a sea of competition.

Take the Nike swoosh, for example. It's one of the most iconic logos in the world. The simplicity of the swoosh, with its sense of motion and speed, perfectly aligns with Nike's brand promise of empowering athletes. Even without the name "Nike" beside it, the swoosh is enough to evoke feelings of performance, victory, and motivation. It's more than just a check mark—it's a visual representation of everything Nike stands for.

On the other hand, brands like Apple use their logo to communicate sleekness, innovation, and minimalism. The bite from the apple is a nod to knowledge and discovery, reflecting Apple's core values of curiosity and pushing boundaries. Over the years, Apple's logo has evolved, but its essence has remained the same: simple, elegant, and forward-thinking. The logo doesn't just represent a tech company—it embodies a brand that encourages creativity and innovation.

But a logo is only as strong as the strategy behind it. It needs to be adaptable, scalable, and timeless. It should look just as good on a billboard as it does on a business card. A poorly designed or overly complicated logo risks alienating potential customers, while a clear, impactful design can leave a lasting impression.

Color psychology: more than just aesthetics

Color is one of the most powerful elements of a brand's visual identity. It can evoke emotion, set the mood, and influence behavior in subtle but significant ways. The right color palette doesn't just make a brand look good; it creates an emotional connection with the audience. This is why brands are careful with their color choices—because each hue carries meaning.

Think about Coca-Cola and its signature red. The color red is often associated with excitement, passion, and energy—qualities that Coca-Cola wants its brand to evoke. When you see that bright red packaging, you instantly recognize it and likely associate it with feelings of joy, fun, and indulgence. Red not only captures attention, but it also builds a sense of brand energy, reinforcing Coca-Cola's positioning as a fun, refreshing beverage.

On the other end of the spectrum, brands like Tiffany & Co. use color to communicate elegance, luxury, and exclusivity. The famous "Tiffany Blue" has become synonymous with sophistication and timeless beauty. Over the years, Tiffany has owned this color so completely that it doesn't need to shout its name—the iconic blue box speaks volumes. Customers don't just purchase jewelry; they purchase the feeling of luxury that Tiffany's visual identity has cultivated.

The psychological impact of color can be profound. Blue, for instance, is often seen as calming and trustworthy, which is why financial institutions like Chase or American Express use shades of blue in their branding. Green, associated with growth, health, and nature, is frequently used by brands like Whole Foods to reinforce their commitment to sustainability and wellness.

When crafting a visual identity, choosing the right color palette is essential. It's not just about what looks good—it's about choosing colors that reflect the brand's personality and values while evoking the desired emotions from the audience.

Typography: giving words a personality

Typography is another key element in a brand's visual identity. The fonts a brand chooses to use, whether in its logo, website, or marketing materials, play a significant role in how it is perceived. Typography can convey authority, playfulness, sophistication, or simplicity, depending on the typeface and how it's used.

For example, Google's simple, modern sans-serif font reflects its mission to make information accessible and user-friendly. The clean lines and lack of ornamentation give off a feeling of approachability and simplicity, which aligns with Google's identity as a tech giant focused on ease of use and innovation.

Contrast that with a luxury brand like Louis Vuitton, which uses classic, serif typography to communicate elegance, tradition, and craftsmanship. The font choice isn't just about aesthetics—it reinforces the brand's heritage and premium positioning. The typography feels refined and timeless, much like the products Louis Vuitton offers.

Choosing the right typography is about more than just picking a font that looks nice. It's about ensuring that the style and tone of the type reflect the brand's overall personality. Is your brand playful and informal? Then a bold, rounded font might suit your identity. Is it serious and authoritative? A classic serif font might be a better fit. Typography gives the brand's voice a visual form, and consistency in typography is essential for creating a cohesive look across all touchpoints.

Visual consistency across all platforms

One of the most important aspects of a successful visual identity is consistency. A brand's visual language should be instantly recognizable, no matter where or how it's encountered. Whether it's on a website, a product package, social media, or an email newsletter, the visual elements must align. Inconsistent use of logos, colors, or fonts can confuse customers and dilute the brand's message.

Apple excels at visual consistency. Whether you're in an Apple store, visiting its website, or watching one of its advertisements, you instantly recognize the brand's minimalist aesthetic. The sleek design, white space, and modern fonts are present across every touchpoint, reinforcing Apple's brand identity of innovation and simplicity.

Consistency doesn't mean being rigid, though. While the core elements of a visual identity—such as logos, colors, and typography—should remain consistent, there should still be room for flexibility to adapt to different platforms or contexts. A brand might use a playful, more casual tone on social media while maintaining a professional image in print. The key is to ensure that even when adapting to different formats, the brand's core identity remains unmistakable.

Beyond the logo: creating a holistic visual language

While logos, colors, and fonts are critical components, a brand's visual identity extends beyond these basic elements. It includes everything from the photography style used in campaigns to the layout of a website, the packaging design, and even the way products are displayed in stores. All of these elements combine to create a cohesive visual language that communicates the brand's message consistently.

IKEA, for instance, has developed a strong visual identity that extends across its catalogs, store layouts, website, and even its product instructions. Everything about the IKEA experience is designed to reflect the brand's essence of affordable, functional design. Its clean, minimalist visuals, use of bold blue and yellow, and simple fonts all work together to create a sense of modernity and practicality. Even its flat-pack furniture instructions, with their iconic line-drawn diagrams, reinforce IKEA's visual language of simplicity and ease.

Brands that think holistically about their visual identity consider every interaction as an opportunity to reinforce their message. Whether it's through packaging, social media graphics, or physical environments, every detail matters. When a brand's visual identity is consistent across all channels, it creates a seamless experience for customers, fostering trust and loyalty.

Creating brand guidelines: consistency across platforms

In a world where brands interact with customers across dozens of platforms—from social media and websites to packaging and in-store experiences—consistency is key. A brand's identity is only as strong as its ability to maintain a cohesive message, tone, and visual style across all touchpoints. This is where brand guidelines come in. Think of them as the brand's rulebook, a set of standards that ensure that no matter where or how customers engage with the brand, they experience the same personality, values, and aesthetic. Brand guidelines protect the integrity of the brand and help avoid a disjointed or confusing customer experience.

Brand guidelines are more than just a set of design rules. They are a strategic tool that provides direction for how a brand presents itself in the marketplace. These guidelines help internal teams, creative agencies, and partners understand how to represent the brand properly, ensuring that every interaction feels authentic and aligned with the brand's essence. Without them, even the strongest brands risk diluting their identity over time.

Why brand guidelines matter

Consistency breeds trust. When customers encounter a brand that looks and sounds the same across all platforms, they come to trust that brand more deeply. Every piece of communication—whether it's a social media post, an email, or product packaging—reinforces the brand's identity and values. Inconsistent messaging, on the other hand, creates confusion, making customers question whether the brand truly knows itself. This can weaken the emotional connection that keeps customers loyal.

Take Coca-Cola, for instance. Whether you see an ad on Instagram, a billboard, or a bottle in the store, you instantly recognize the brand. Coca-Cola's iconic red, signature script, and consistent use of imagery centered around happiness and togetherness all work together to form a cohesive, instantly recognizable brand experience. This didn't happen by chance—it's the result of strict adherence to brand guidelines that have been refined over decades.

Brand guidelines also play a crucial role internally. When teams understand the brand's rules, they're empowered to create content and experiences that feel unified, regardless of who's behind the work. Without guidelines, even well-intentioned efforts can lead to mixed messages, inconsistent visuals, or tone-deaf communication.

The elements of effective brand guidelines

Effective brand guidelines cover a broad range of elements that together create a brand's identity. While the exact details vary from brand to brand, these guidelines typically include core components such as logo usage, color palettes, typography, tone of voice, and imagery styles. Each element contributes to how the brand is perceived and how it differentiates itself from competitors.

At the heart of brand guidelines is the **logo**. A good set of guidelines will outline exactly how the logo should be used—and, just as importantly, how it shouldn't be used. This includes rules about spacing, sizing, and placement, as well as acceptable variations of the logo (for example, black and white versions or simplified marks for smaller formats). The goal is to protect the integrity of the logo, ensuring that it remains consistent and recognizable across all touchpoints.

Color palette is another essential component. Colors evoke emotion and set the mood for how a brand is experienced. Brand guidelines provide a set of approved colors, often including primary and secondary palettes. These colors are carefully chosen to represent the brand's personality and should be used consistently in marketing materials, product packaging, and digital platforms. A company like Spotify, for example, has maintained a signature shade of green, which has become synonymous with its brand. By sticking to this color consistently, Spotify has created strong visual recognition across its platforms.

Typography is another key part of brand guidelines. The fonts a brand chooses to use communicate its tone and values. For example, a bold, modern font may convey innovation and forward-thinking, while a classic serif font might communicate tradition and reliability. Brand guidelines provide rules for font usage, including when and where certain typefaces should be used. This ensures that everything from a website's header to a printed brochure feels like it belongs to the same brand.

Brand guidelines don't stop at design. **Tone of voice** is a critical element in how a brand communicates. A brand's voice is how it sounds when it "speaks" to its audience—whether that's in a tweet, an email, or a product description. Guidelines around tone help keep the brand's personality consistent. For example, if a brand has a friendly and casual tone, its emails, social media posts, and website copy should all reflect that same approachable vibe. On the flip side, a brand that aims to be authoritative and expert-driven needs to maintain that tone across all channels to build credibility.

Imagery and photography guidelines are equally important, especially for brands that rely heavily on visual storytelling. These guidelines outline the style of photography or illustrations that should be used, whether it's high-contrast, minimalist, or lifestyle-focused. Brands like Airbnb use warm, inviting imagery in all their communications to reflect the human-centered experience of travel and connection. By staying consistent with this style, Airbnb ensures that all visuals reflect the brand's essence of belonging.

Flexibility within guidelines

While consistency is crucial, brand guidelines also need to be flexible enough to adapt to new platforms, formats, and contexts. A good set of guidelines strikes a balance between maintaining the integrity of the brand and allowing for creative expression. For example, while a brand's tone might be friendly and conversational across most channels, it may need to be more formal in investor reports or technical documentation. The key is to keep the core essence intact while adapting to different audiences.

Nike's brand guidelines are a great example of flexibility. While Nike's core identity—focused on performance, empowerment, and motivation—remains constant, the brand's visual and tonal expression can shift depending on the platform. Nike's website might have a sleek, modern feel, while its social media is more playful and engaging, designed to interact with younger audiences. Despite these variations, the underlying brand personality always shines through.

Keeping teams aligned

Brand guidelines aren't just a document to reference—they're a tool for alignment. As brands grow and teams expand, having clear guidelines ensures that everyone—from designers and marketers to product developers and social media managers—understands how to represent the brand. This becomes especially important for global brands with regional teams, where maintaining consistency across cultures and markets can be challenging.

For instance, global companies like Starbucks need to ensure that their brand identity remains consistent whether you're visiting a store in Seattle or Singapore. Starbucks' brand guidelines ensure that every location feels familiar, with the same tone of voice, logo usage, and visual identity. Yet, they allow for some regional adaptations, such as menu items that cater to local tastes or in-store designs that reflect cultural influences. The result is a brand that feels consistent globally but still relevant locally.

The importance of regular updates

As brands evolve, so should their guidelines. New platforms emerge, customer expectations shift, and design trends change. Regularly updating brand guidelines ensures that the brand stays relevant without losing its core identity. This doesn't mean overhauling the brand's visual identity every year—far from it. Instead, it's about making strategic adjustments that allow the brand to grow while staying true to its essence.

For example, when Instagram first launched, many brands didn't have specific guidelines for how their logos or imagery should be used on such a highly visual platform. But as social media grew in importance, brands like Adidas and Coca-Cola updated their guidelines to include rules for creating consistent and engaging visual content across these new platforms. By staying ahead of trends, these brands maintained their relevance and strengthened their presence.

Protecting the brand's integrity

Inconsistent branding is more than just a cosmetic issue—it can erode trust and weaken the brand's impact. Customers expect a consistent experience, whether they're engaging with the brand online, in-store, or through advertising. Brand guidelines protect the brand's integrity by ensuring that every interaction, no matter the platform, reinforces the same core message and aesthetic.

Companies like Google have used their brand guidelines to create a cohesive identity that is instantly recognizable, even as their product offerings expand. Whether it's the clean design of their search engine, the user-friendly interfaces of Google Docs, or the playfulness of Google Doodles, the brand's visual and tonal consistency has helped it maintain a strong and unified presence.

Brand voice vs. brand tone: what's the difference?

In the world of branding, the terms "voice" and "tone" are often used interchangeably. However, they represent two distinct elements of how a brand communicates with its audience. Both brand voice and brand tone are crucial for building a recognizable and trustworthy brand personality, but they serve different purposes. Understanding the difference—and how to use them together effectively—can make or break how your brand connects with its customers.

Think of brand voice as your brand's personality. It's consistent and unchanging, the defining character of how your brand expresses itself. On the other hand, tone is adaptable. It's the way your brand's voice comes across depending on the situation or context, changing subtly depending on who you're speaking to, what platform you're on, or what's happening in the world.

Voice is the **what**, while tone is the **how**.

Defining brand voice: the foundation of your brand's personality

Brand voice is the foundation of all your brand's communication. It's the distinctive way your brand speaks, shaped by your core values, mission, and essence. A brand's voice is what makes it unique and memorable—it doesn't change, regardless of the platform, audience, or situation. Whether you're writing an Instagram caption, responding to a customer query, or creating a TV commercial, the brand voice stays the same.

For example, Mailchimp has a voice that is friendly, quirky, and a little humorous. This consistent voice is present in everything they do, from their website copy to their customer service interactions. It helps make the brand approachable, even when dealing with a more complex product like email marketing automation.

Mailchimp's voice is instantly recognizable and builds trust because it feels familiar and authentic.

Voice doesn't just shape how a brand communicates—it also helps shape how it's perceived. Nike's brand voice, for instance, is bold and empowering. Whether it's in an ad campaign or on social media, Nike speaks with the same voice of motivation and confidence. This consistency reinforces the brand's identity as one that inspires athletes to push their limits, regardless of the medium.

Brand tone: adapting to the moment

While voice stays constant, tone shifts depending on the situation. Tone is how the brand voice is expressed in different contexts. It adjusts to match the mood, platform, or audience. A brand might have a playful tone on social media but adopt a more formal tone in a press release or an annual report. The key is that the tone changes, but the underlying voice remains the same.

Think of tone as the volume knob on your brand's voice. Sometimes, it's light and conversational; other times, it's more serious or professional. But no matter the tone, the voice stays true to the brand's personality.

Take Starbucks as an example. The brand's voice is warm, friendly, and community-focused, reflecting its mission of being the "third place" between home and work. However, the tone changes based on the context. On social media, Starbucks might use a light, upbeat tone to engage with followers, posting pictures of seasonal drinks with casual, inviting captions. In a corporate communication, such as an environmental sustainability report, the tone would shift to be more formal and responsible, yet the core voice—community and connection—remains.

How voice and tone work together

For a brand to maintain its integrity and build trust with its audience, voice and tone need to work in harmony. The voice is the personality that customers recognize and relate to, while the tone adjusts the way that personality comes across based on what the brand is saying, who it's speaking to, or where the message is being delivered.

Consistency in voice builds familiarity, while flexibility in tone helps brands navigate different conversations and contexts without losing their core identity. A brand that is too rigid in tone across all platforms risks coming across as disconnected or tone-deaf. On the other hand, a brand that changes its voice too often loses credibility and confuses its audience.

Think of Netflix, a brand that has mastered the balance of voice and tone. Its voice is casual, witty, and inclusive, making Netflix feel like a friend who always knows the best shows to recommend. On Twitter, Netflix's tone is fun and irreverent, often using memes or pop culture references to engage with users. But when announcing serious decisions, like pricing changes or new policies, the tone shifts to be more straightforward and respectful, while still maintaining the brand's approachable voice. This balance allows Netflix to stay consistent, even when the message or mood changes.

Finding the right balance for your brand

To successfully navigate between voice and tone, brands need to have a clear understanding of who they are and who they're speaking to. Voice should be rooted in the brand's essence, values, and mission, while tone should be adaptable to fit the context. The challenge is finding the right balance—knowing when to be lighthearted and when to be serious, when to be formal and when to be conversational.

Consider Slack, a brand whose voice is friendly, efficient, and focused on productivity. The tone Slack uses in different contexts varies. For onboarding tutorials, the tone is instructional but still casual, helping users feel at ease as they learn the platform. In customer support, the tone is empathetic and helpful, offering solutions while maintaining the same approachable, human voice. This flexibility allows Slack to communicate effectively without losing its core identity as a helpful tool for workplace communication.

The risks of inconsistency

When brands fail to balance voice and tone, it can lead to confusion or, worse, a loss of trust. Imagine a brand with a professional, authoritative voice suddenly adopting a highly informal tone in a serious context—it would feel off, as though the brand isn't being true to itself. This dissonance can erode customer trust, making the brand seem less reliable or even insincere.

A famous example of this comes from the luxury fashion brand Burberry, which for a time struggled with an identity crisis. Known for its high-end, classic British style, Burberry tried to appeal to a younger audience by loosening its tone and voice in marketing, which caused a disconnect with its core customers. The attempt to change voice confused both loyal and new customers, and Burberry eventually had to refocus on its heritage to restore its brand's reputation.

On the flip side, being too rigid with tone can make a brand feel out of touch. During sensitive times—such as social or political crises—brands that don't adapt their tone can come across as tone-deaf. For example, during the COVID-19 pandemic, many brands had to adjust their typically upbeat and promotional tones to acknowledge the seriousness of the situation. Brands like Airbnb did this effectively, shifting their tone to emphasize empathy and understanding, while still maintaining their voice centered around community and belonging.

Creating guidelines for voice and tone

Establishing clear guidelines for brand voice and tone is essential for maintaining consistency while allowing for flexibility. These guidelines should outline the brand's core voice—its personality, values, and the emotions it wants to evoke—and provide examples of how tone can shift depending on the context.

For instance, a company might define its voice as "friendly, knowledgeable, and helpful," but explain that the tone should shift from casual in social media to professional in formal presentations. Guidelines ensure that everyone—from social media managers to copywriters to customer service reps—uses the brand's voice consistently while adapting tone to the situation at hand.

By clearly defining voice and tone, brands can maintain a unified identity across all channels and touchpoints. This not only creates a more cohesive brand experience but also strengthens the emotional connection with customers, who come to recognize and trust the brand's unique personality.

Building a cohesive brand personality through visual and verbal expression

A brand's personality isn't just what it says; it's also how it looks. The combination of visual identity and verbal expression creates a brand's full personality, forming the foundation for how it connects with its audience. While each of these elements plays its own role, they need to work together seamlessly for a brand to feel consistent, authentic, and recognizable across all touchpoints. A brand that can successfully align its visual and verbal identity is more than just a logo or a slogan—it becomes something customers can relate to, trust, and even love.

In an era where consumers are bombarded with options and messages, brand personality is often the deciding factor in how people make choices. When both visual and verbal elements reinforce the same core identity, the brand creates a powerful impression. Brands like Apple, Nike, and Starbucks excel at this—when you think of them, you don't just think of a product; you think of an experience, a feeling, a story.

The power of alignment: creating a unified personality

A cohesive brand personality starts with alignment. Every visual and verbal touchpoint should reflect the same core essence, from the fonts and colors on a website to the tone of voice in customer emails. This doesn't mean everything has to be identical; rather, each element should feel like a natural extension of the brand's personality.

Apple is an excellent example of this alignment in action. Apple's verbal expression—clear, simple, and innovative—is perfectly mirrored in its visual identity, which is clean, minimalistic, and sleek. The brand's messaging is never overloaded with jargon or excessive detail, just as its design aesthetic avoids clutter and distraction. Whether you're looking at a billboard, using an iPhone, or navigating the Apple website, the brand's personality remains consistent: forward-thinking, user-friendly, and elegant. The synergy between Apple's visual and verbal identity reinforces its brand values at every turn, creating a cohesive personality that customers trust and admire.

When verbal and visual expression aren't aligned, the brand's identity feels fractured, leaving customers confused. Imagine a luxury brand that uses a refined, sophisticated logo but communicates with slang-filled, casual language. This disconnect weakens the brand's identity, diluting its perceived value. For customers to build emotional connections with brands, they need to feel consistency in both how the brand looks and sounds.

The role of visual identity: expressing personality through design

Visual identity is the most immediate way a brand communicates. Long before someone reads a tagline or hears an ad, they encounter the visual representation of the brand—its logo, colors, typography, and overall design language. These elements form a crucial part of the brand's personality, shaping first impressions and setting expectations.

Take Tiffany & Co., whose famous Tiffany Blue is as much a part of its personality as its messaging around timeless elegance and luxury. The color has become synonymous with the brand's high-end jewelry, evoking feelings of sophistication and class. Tiffany's visual identity—its minimalist logo, classic fonts, and restrained use of color—creates a cohesive look that reflects the brand's essence. It feels luxurious without being ostentatious, which aligns with the way the brand communicates verbally: confident, elegant, and understated.

Visual identity is more than just aesthetics—it's a strategic tool for conveying values and emotions. For example, bold colors and dynamic typography can signal energy and innovation, while softer tones and traditional fonts evoke calm and reliability. Brands like Google, with its vibrant primary color palette and playful logo design, use visual elements to reinforce its identity as approachable, creative, and open.

While logos and colors often get the most attention, other visual cues—like photography style, packaging, and layout—are equally important in shaping how customers perceive a brand. These visual elements should consistently reflect the same personality traits as the verbal expression. If the visual identity tells one story but the verbal messaging tells another, the disconnect can leave customers unsure about what the brand really stands for.

The power of words: shaping perception through verbal identity

Verbal identity—how a brand speaks—is just as important as how it looks. A brand's tone of voice, choice of words, and messaging all contribute to how its personality is perceived. Whether it's through a tagline, a tweet, or a customer service response, the language a brand uses helps define who it is and what it stands for.

Consider the way Ben & Jerry's communicates. Its verbal identity is fun, quirky, and authentic, using casual, lighthearted language that makes the brand feel approachable. But there's more to the personality than just humor—Ben & Jerry's also uses its voice to speak out on social and environmental issues, reinforcing its values of social justice and sustainability. This consistency in tone builds trust with its audience, allowing the brand to be both playful and serious when the moment calls for it. The result is a brand that feels real, like a friend who knows when to make you laugh and when to take a stand.

Verbal identity also needs to adapt to different contexts while staying true to the brand's core personality. A brand might use a more formal tone when communicating through press releases but adopt a casual, conversational tone on social media. The key is that both tones still reflect the same personality. Slack, for instance, maintains a friendly and efficient voice across its communications, but the tone shifts slightly depending on whether it's helping onboard new users or addressing technical issues in customer support.

By clearly defining its verbal identity, a brand can ensure that every piece of communication feels authentic and aligned with its personality. This clarity makes it easier for customers to connect with the brand, knowing what to expect each time they engage.

Bringing it all together: crafting a cohesive experience

Building a cohesive brand personality through both visual and verbal expression requires more than just strong design or clever copywriting. It's about creating an experience where every interaction with the brand feels like part of the same story. From the way a product is packaged to how a brand responds on social media, every detail contributes to the overall perception of the brand.

Look at Nike's storytelling. Nike's visuals—bold typography, dynamic imagery, and striking use of contrast—reflect the energy and drive of its brand voice, which is all about pushing limits and inspiring greatness. When you watch a Nike commercial or scroll through its Instagram feed, the words, images, and design work in unison to create a single, powerful message: Just Do It. Nike doesn't just tell you about empowerment; it shows it visually through action shots of athletes in motion, paired with powerful, motivational language. This alignment between visual and verbal expression is what makes Nike's brand personality so strong and impactful.

For brands to build this kind of cohesiveness, they need clear guidelines that define both their visual and verbal identity. These guidelines help ensure that everyone—whether they're designing a website, creating social content, or drafting an email—represents the brand consistently. But it's also important to leave room for flexibility. The tone of voice or visual style might adapt slightly depending on the platform or audience, but the core identity should remain unmistakable.

The emotional connection: why it matters

When visual and verbal expression are aligned, they don't just create a brand that looks good—they create a brand that feels good. Customers respond emotionally to brands that have a strong personality, because they feel like they're engaging with something more human. Whether it's a luxury brand that makes customers feel sophisticated or a tech company that inspires creativity, the emotional connection is what turns casual buyers into loyal fans.

Take Coca-Cola. The brand's personality, expressed through both its iconic red-and-white color scheme and its messaging about happiness and togetherness, evokes a specific emotional response. Coca-Cola's visual elements—warm, nostalgic imagery and classic design—complement its verbal messaging about sharing moments with loved ones. This consistency across both visual and verbal cues is what makes Coca-Cola a symbol of joy and celebration around the world.

Ultimately, the goal of building a cohesive brand personality is to make every interaction with the brand feel like part of a larger story. When a customer sees your logo, reads your tagline, or opens your packaging, they should feel a connection that goes beyond the product or service itself. It's this connection that makes a brand memorable, trustworthy, and, most importantly, loved.

The role of emotion in brand expression: making people feel, not just think

In the crowded marketplace of today, logic alone doesn't drive brand loyalty—emotion does. While rational decisions about price, features, and convenience matter, it's how a brand makes people feel that creates lasting connections. A brand that can tap into emotion, making customers feel something meaningful, will stand out. Emotional branding transforms a transactional relationship into a personal one, building loyalty that goes beyond product satisfaction.

Successful brands understand that buying decisions are often emotional first and logical second. The strongest brand expressions—whether through visuals, tone, or storytelling—don't just give consumers something to think about, they make them feel something. This emotional pull is what turns customers into advocates, creating a deeper, more resilient connection.

The power of emotional triggers

Brands that evoke emotion understand how to tap into universal feelings like joy, nostalgia, fear, or hope. These emotional triggers not only grab attention but also make the brand more memorable. When a brand can make people feel happy, inspired, or understood, it creates a positive association that lingers long after the product is purchased or the service is used.

Consider Coca-Cola's long-standing strategy of connecting its brand to happiness. The iconic *Open Happiness* campaign is a great example of emotional branding in action. Coca-Cola isn't selling just a soft drink; it's selling a moment of joy, celebration, and togetherness. Whether it's a family gathering or friends sharing a Coke at a summer BBQ, the brand has woven itself into the fabric of life's happiest moments. The drink becomes secondary—the emotion of happiness and connection is what stays with the consumer.

This is the essence of emotional branding. Instead of focusing on the functional aspects of the product, Coca-Cola's marketing puts joy front and center. The emotional resonance is so strong that the brand has become synonymous with happiness, making it a global cultural icon.

Visual identity: evoking emotion through design

Visual elements are a powerful tool for stirring emotions. Color, imagery, and design can convey feelings before a single word is spoken. The colors a brand chooses can evoke calm, excitement, trust, or even urgency. Think of how the color blue is used in many tech and finance brands to communicate reliability and professionalism, while warm colors like red and orange stir excitement or passion.

A great example of visual identity driving emotion is Airbnb. The brand's color palette is warm and inviting, with soft tones that evoke a sense of comfort and safety. This visual warmth is further supported by its imagery, which often features real people, authentic homes, and heartfelt interactions between hosts and guests. The effect is immediate: Airbnb doesn't just offer places to stay, it offers experiences that feel personal, welcoming, and full of connection.

Even the design of a brand's logo can carry emotional weight. The Nike swoosh, for instance, is more than just a logo—it's a symbol of movement, victory, and empowerment. The simplicity and dynamism of the design create a feeling of momentum and ambition, perfectly aligning with the brand's message of *Just Do It*. The logo itself stirs emotion, inspiring athletes and consumers alike to push beyond their limits.

Storytelling: tapping into emotional narratives

Storytelling is one of the most effective ways for brands to evoke emotion. A well-crafted story engages both the heart and the mind, making the brand relatable and human. Instead of bombarding consumers with features or facts, emotional storytelling allows brands to connect on a deeper level by focusing on shared experiences, challenges, or aspirations.

Take Dove's *Real Beauty* campaign as an example. Rather than highlighting the functional benefits of its products, Dove focuses on redefining beauty standards and encouraging women to embrace their natural beauty. The campaign is built around real, unretouched images of women, along with heartfelt stories of self-acceptance. By doing this, Dove doesn't just sell beauty products—it taps into a broader cultural conversation, creating an emotional bond with consumers who see themselves reflected in the campaign's message of inclusivity and confidence.

The strength of Dove's approach lies in its authenticity. The brand's storytelling feels genuine, and the emotion it evokes—pride, empowerment, and self-love—resonates with its target audience. Consumers aren't just buying a bar of soap; they're buying into a message that makes them feel seen and valued.

Tone of voice: creating emotional resonance through language

A brand's tone of voice plays a huge role in how it makes people feel. The words a brand chooses, the rhythm of its sentences, and the warmth (or coolness) of its language all contribute to how it connects emotionally. A playful, upbeat tone can make a brand feel fun and accessible, while a more serious tone can instill trust and credibility. But whatever tone is used, it must reflect the brand's essence and values to build genuine connections.

Take Apple's tone of voice as an example. In its marketing, Apple's language is simple, clear, and direct. There's no fluff—just clean, concise messaging that makes customers feel empowered and smart. Apple focuses on showing how its products will improve your life, but it does so without talking down to its audience. This tone fosters a sense of empowerment, making customers feel that they are in control, and that the brand understands their needs.

In contrast, brands like Ben & Jerry's use a more playful, lighthearted tone, often blending humor with social activism. The brand's whimsical product names and cheeky website copy create a sense of joy, making the buying experience fun while reinforcing Ben & Jerry's quirky, socially conscious personality. It's not just about the ice cream—it's about making you smile and feel good about the values behind the product.

The emotional impact of user-generated content

In many cases, the most emotionally powerful content comes directly from customers themselves. User-generated content, such as customer reviews, social media posts, or video testimonials, adds authenticity to a brand's emotional appeal. When customers share their experiences, the stories feel real and relatable, making it easier for potential customers to connect emotionally.

Brands like Glossier have built entire communities around user-generated content. By encouraging customers to share their beauty routines and product experiences, Glossier amplifies the emotional connection with its audience. Real people, with real skin concerns and successes, create stories that feel personal and authentic. This type of content stirs emotions like trust, confidence, and relatability, allowing Glossier to stand out in a crowded beauty market.

User-generated content taps into the idea of social proof, where customers trust the opinions of their peers more than traditional advertising. These stories are emotionally charged because they are personal, making it easier for other customers to imagine themselves having similar positive experiences.

Building loyalty through emotional branding

Brands that succeed in making emotional connections with their audience often enjoy stronger customer loyalty. When consumers feel an emotional attachment to a brand, they are more likely to stick with it, even if competitors offer similar products or lower prices. This emotional loyalty is what turns casual buyers into lifelong customers and advocates.

Consider the loyalty that brands like Harley-Davidson inspire. Harley's entire brand is built around freedom, rebellion, and individuality—emotions that resonate deeply with its core audience. The brand's messaging, design, and even its community events all reinforce this emotional connection, turning customers into passionate advocates who see Harley as more than just a motorcycle company—it's a lifestyle.

This emotional loyalty often extends beyond products. Customers are not just buying what the brand sells—they are buying the emotions, values, and experiences that come with it. Brands that consistently evoke positive emotions can create customer relationships that go beyond the transactional, ensuring long-term success in a competitive market.

Brand expression across different platforms

In today's digital age, brands are constantly interacting with their audience across a variety of platforms—from social media and websites to email, print, and physical spaces. Each of these platforms comes with its own set of rules, formats, and audience expectations. Successfully adapting your brand's expression to fit these platforms while staying true to your core identity is both a challenge and an opportunity. Brands that can master this balance build stronger, more authentic connections with their audience, while those that fail risk losing consistency and trust.

The key to brand expression across platforms is flexibility within a framework. Your brand's core identity—its mission, values, personality, and voice—should always remain consistent. However, the way that identity is expressed may shift depending on the platform, ensuring the message resonates with the specific audience and medium.

The challenge of platform adaptation

Each platform offers a unique way for brands to communicate with their audience. Social media, for example, is often informal, quick, and visually driven, while email marketing demands a more direct, informative approach. Websites are interactive, with a focus on user experience, while print materials often lean heavily on design and longer-form content. Adapting your brand expression to these different contexts requires an understanding of each platform's nuances and the expectations of the audience using them.

Take Instagram, for example. On this visually oriented platform, brands like Glossier thrive by using clean, minimal visuals and short, snappy captions that feel personal and relatable. Their use of user-generated content and a conversational tone makes the brand feel accessible. Glossier stays true to its identity as a beauty brand that's built around simplicity and community, but the tone and style are adapted to fit the quick, visual nature of Instagram.

In contrast, LinkedIn is more formal and professional. Here, brands need to shift their tone to align with the platform's business-oriented audience. A company like IBM, for example, will focus on thought leadership, technology trends, and industry insights when communicating on LinkedIn, using a tone that reflects expertise and authority. However, the brand's core identity—focused on innovation and technology—remains intact, even though the expression changes to fit the platform's expectations.

Visual consistency with platform flexibility

Maintaining visual consistency across platforms is one of the most important aspects of brand expression. While the layout, size, or format might change depending on the platform, the core visual elements—like logos, color schemes, typography, and imagery—

should stay consistent. This ensures that customers can easily recognize the brand, no matter where they encounter it.

Coca-Cola, for instance, has a globally recognized visual identity. Whether you see an ad on a billboard, a post on Instagram, or a promotional email, the brand's signature red, flowing script logo, and imagery of people enjoying Coca-Cola in social settings remain constant. However, Coca-Cola adapts its visuals to suit the platform's strengths. On Instagram, the brand uses bright, eye-catching images that pop on a small screen, while in print, it might focus on storytelling through more detailed, nostalgic imagery. The adaptability lies in how the brand uses its visuals, not in changing the visuals themselves.

Consistency doesn't mean being rigid. Brands need to be mindful of each platform's unique design constraints. For instance, a website's layout may allow for a detailed, interactive experience, while a Twitter post requires brands to communicate their message in just a few words and a single image. The trick is to maintain the core elements that make the brand recognizable while tailoring the expression to suit the platform's strengths.

Tone of voice: speaking the language of each platform

A brand's tone of voice should adapt to fit the platform without losing the brand's personality. The way a brand speaks on Twitter is likely to be more casual and concise than how it communicates in a corporate press release, but the underlying voice—whether it's playful, authoritative, or empathetic—should be the same.

Netflix is a brand that exemplifies this balance. On Twitter, Netflix's tone is witty, conversational, and sometimes irreverent, creating a sense of fun and engagement with its audience. It uses memes, pop culture references, and humorous replies to make the brand feel relatable. On its website, however, Netflix shifts to a more straightforward tone, focusing on ease of use and discovery. The humor may take a back seat, but the friendly, user-first approach remains.

This adaptability in tone is crucial for building rapport with different audience segments. Social media users expect quick, conversational exchanges, while email subscribers might look for more detailed, informative content. By adjusting the tone but keeping the voice consistent, brands can meet audience expectations while reinforcing their personality.

Tailoring content without losing identity

Another challenge of brand expression across platforms is tailoring content while staying true to your brand's core message. For example, a luxury brand like Louis Vuitton needs to maintain its high-end, exclusive image, whether it's communicating through a glossy magazine ad or a tweet. The language, visuals, and overall messaging need to reflect luxury, craftsmanship, and status, even when adapted for different platforms.

On Instagram, Louis Vuitton might focus on visually striking images of its latest collections, paired with minimal text, allowing the product to speak for itself. On its website, the brand can go deeper, offering detailed descriptions of its products, the craftsmanship involved, and the heritage behind the designs. The platform changes, but the brand's expression—focused on luxury and elegance—remains consistent.

The key is to adapt the depth and focus of the content without compromising the brand's core values. For example, while a brand might highlight product features on a website, the same message on Twitter needs to be condensed, with a sharper focus on engaging the audience quickly. The message is simplified, but the core identity remains intact.

Staying consistent across cultures

For global brands, adapting across platforms also means considering different cultural contexts. What works on social media in the United States may not resonate in Japan or Brazil. Brands must be mindful of cultural differences while ensuring that their global identity remains consistent.

McDonald's is a brand that excels at this balance. Globally, McDonald's maintains a consistent identity of fun, family-friendly fast food, but the way it expresses this identity varies by region. In Japan, McDonald's advertisements focus on sleek design and innovation, aligning with local tastes for high-quality, well-presented products. In the United States, the brand emphasizes nostalgia and indulgence, with campaigns focusing on classic menu items like the Big Mac. The core identity—affordable, accessible comfort food—remains the same, but the expression adapts to local expectations.

Maintaining brand integrity across new platforms

As new platforms emerge, brands need to be agile enough to adapt while maintaining their identity. Whether it's experimenting with TikTok's short-form video content or diving into the immersive world of virtual reality, brands that can express themselves authentically in new environments gain a competitive edge.

Take Nike's foray into TikTok. The brand stays true to its core message of empowerment and athleticism but tailors its content to TikTok's fast-paced, creative platform. Instead of traditional ads, Nike leverages user-generated content, challenges, and short videos that feel authentic to the TikTok audience. This allows Nike to remain relevant in a rapidly changing digital landscape without sacrificing the integrity of its brand.

The importance of brand guidelines

To ensure consistency across platforms, brand guidelines are essential. These guidelines provide the framework for how a brand should be expressed visually and verbally, no matter where it's seen. They ensure that every piece of content—from an email to a billboard—feels cohesive and true to the brand's identity. While guidelines set the boundaries, they also allow for flexibility in how the brand can adapt to different contexts.

Brands like Starbucks use comprehensive guidelines to maintain consistency across their global operations. Whether it's a store in London or a social media campaign in Brazil, the visual and verbal identity of Starbucks remains consistent. The color schemes, typography, tone, and even the in-store experience all align with the brand's core essence of community and comfort, while allowing for local adaptations.

CHAPTER 04
THE FOURTH E

Experience

Crafting a seamless brand experience across touchpoints

In today's hyper-connected world, customers interact with brands across an ever-expanding array of touchpoints. From websites and social media to in-store experiences and customer service interactions, every encounter a customer has with your brand contributes to their overall perception of it. The brands that win aren't necessarily those with the best products, but those that create a seamless, consistent experience at every stage of the customer journey. Crafting a unified brand experience across all touchpoints isn't just about ensuring consistency—it's about building trust, loyalty, and emotional connections with your audience.

A seamless brand experience means that every interaction feels connected and cohesive, no matter the platform or medium. Whether a customer is browsing your website, scrolling through your Instagram feed, or speaking with your customer service team, they should feel like they're engaging with the same brand. This sense of continuity reinforces your brand's identity and makes customers feel understood and valued, turning everyday interactions into meaningful experiences.

Why a seamless experience matters

Customer expectations have shifted. In the past, a customer might interact with a brand through just a few channels—perhaps visiting a store or browsing a catalog. Today, however, they're likely engaging through multiple touchpoints, often simultaneously. They might research a product on their phone, read reviews online, check prices on a desktop, and ultimately make a purchase in-store. If these touchpoints feel disjointed or disconnected, the customer's experience can suffer, leading to frustration or even lost sales.

A seamless brand experience ensures that customers have a smooth, consistent journey no matter how or where they engage with your brand. This consistency builds trust. When customers encounter the same voice, tone, and visual elements across platforms, it reinforces your brand's reliability and professionalism. A consistent experience also enhances recall—making it easier for customers to remember and recognize your brand amidst a sea of competitors.

Apple is a prime example of a brand that has mastered the art of creating a seamless experience. Whether you're using their products, visiting an Apple Store, or interacting with their customer service, the experience is consistent. Apple's sleek, minimalist design language carries through from their physical products to their website, app interfaces, and packaging. Even the in-store experience feels cohesive, with clean lines, open spaces, and knowledgeable staff offering the same high-quality experience as Apple's digital platforms. This consistency across touchpoints not only enhances brand loyalty but also sets clear expectations for customers, who know exactly what kind of experience they're getting every time they engage with Apple.

Connecting online and offline experiences

One of the biggest challenges in crafting a seamless brand experience is ensuring continuity between online and offline interactions. In a world where e-commerce and digital experiences are growing rapidly, many brands struggle to align their physical and digital presences. However, the brands that succeed in integrating these experiences create a sense of continuity that enhances customer satisfaction.

Nike is a brand that has successfully bridged the gap between its online and offline experiences. Through its Nike app and website, customers can research products, place orders, and even book in-store pickup. When they visit a physical store, they can use the app to scan items for more information or check availability in other locations. Nike's online and offline touchpoints work together seamlessly, providing a consistent, omnichannel experience that makes shopping more convenient and personalized.

For brands that operate both online and in physical spaces, it's essential to create a seamless handoff between these environments. Whether it's offering options like "buy online, pick up in-store" or ensuring that in-store staff have access to the same customer data as online channels, brands that integrate these touchpoints provide a more cohesive experience. This integration helps customers feel like they're dealing with a single entity, rather than two disconnected worlds.

Maintaining consistency across platforms

Another important aspect of crafting a seamless brand experience is maintaining consistency across different digital platforms. Brands today engage with their audience on websites, social media, email newsletters, apps, and beyond. Each platform may have its own unique format, but the experience should feel unified.

Consistency goes beyond using the same logo or colors—it's about ensuring that your brand's voice, values, and tone come through clearly on every platform. Brands like Starbucks have mastered this. Whether you're browsing their website, scrolling through their Instagram feed, or receiving an email, the tone remains warm, welcoming, and focused on community. Starbucks' iconic green color and simple, earthy aesthetic are ever-present, reinforcing the brand's essence at every touchpoint.

While each platform serves a different purpose, the experience should still feel cohesive. For example, the casual, image-driven nature of Instagram allows for more playful and visually engaging content, while email newsletters may require a more detailed and informative tone. The key is to adapt to the platform without sacrificing the brand's overall identity. Customers should feel like they're dealing with the same brand, even as the format and style shift.

Personalization: Making the experience feel unique

While consistency is essential, a seamless brand experience goes beyond standardization—it also needs to feel personal. Customers today expect brands to deliver experiences that cater to their individual needs, preferences, and behavior. This means going beyond simply offering a uniform experience and creating one that feels tailored to each person.

Amazon is a leader in this area, using data to personalize nearly every aspect of the customer experience. From personalized product recommendations to targeted emails based on past purchases, Amazon makes each interaction feel like it's designed specifically for the individual. This level of personalization not only enhances customer satisfaction but also drives loyalty, as customers feel like the brand truly understands them.

The key to successful personalization lies in using data intelligently. Whether it's tracking customer behavior on your website, analyzing purchase history, or using CRM systems to manage customer interactions, the more you understand about your customers, the better you can tailor the experience to meet their needs. Brands that get personalization right build stronger emotional connections with their audience, as customers feel seen and valued rather than just another number.

Creating emotional consistency

Crafting a seamless brand experience isn't just about technical or visual consistency—it's about emotional consistency, too. Every touchpoint should reinforce the feelings your brand aims to evoke, whether that's excitement, trust, comfort, or innovation. Customers shouldn't feel one way when they visit your store and another when they interact with your brand online. Instead, the emotional experience should be consistent across all channels.

Take Disney, for example. Disney's entire brand is built around the concept of magic and wonder, and this emotional experience is carried through every interaction. Whether guests are visiting a theme park, watching a movie, or interacting with the Disney+ streaming service, they are enveloped in a sense of adventure and joy. This consistency in emotional experience helps create a deeper connection between the brand and its audience, fostering loyalty that spans generations.

Brands that want to create emotional consistency need to define the feelings they want to evoke and ensure that every touchpoint reinforces those emotions. This requires careful attention to both the language and visuals used in each platform, as well as how customer interactions are managed. The goal is to make every experience feel like a continuation of the same emotional journey.

Sensory branding: Engaging consumers beyond sight and sound

Branding is often thought of in terms of what we see and hear—logos, colors, music, and slogans. But truly memorable brands go beyond these basics, tapping into all five senses to create a deeper, more immersive experience. Sensory branding engages consumers on a multi-sensory level, making the brand feel more tangible and personal. By stimulating not just sight and sound but also touch, taste, and smell, brands can trigger stronger emotional responses, build lasting memories, and forge deeper connections with their audience.

Humans process the world through their senses, and when multiple senses are engaged simultaneously, the experience becomes more vivid and memorable. Sensory branding is about activating these different sensory pathways in a way that reinforces a brand's identity and enhances the overall customer experience. Whether it's the feel of high-quality packaging, the scent of a store, or the taste of a signature product, sensory branding invites consumers to experience the brand with more than just their eyes and ears.

The power of smell: creating lasting impressions

Of all the senses, smell is perhaps the most powerful in triggering memories and emotions. Research shows that people are 100 times more likely to remember something they smell than something they see, hear, or touch. This makes scent a particularly valuable tool for brands looking to create long-lasting emotional connections with their audience.

One of the most successful examples of sensory branding through smell comes from Abercrombie & Fitch. For years, the brand famously infused its stores with its signature fragrance, Fierce. The scent became so closely associated with the brand that it would trigger instant recognition, even outside the store. The fragrance acted as an olfactory signature, building a sensory connection that reinforced Abercrombie's youthful, energetic, and aspirational brand identity.

Scent branding isn't limited to retail spaces. Companies like Westin Hotels have embraced sensory branding by introducing signature scents in their lobbies. Westin's "White Tea" fragrance creates a calming, luxurious atmosphere, reinforcing the brand's focus on relaxation and well-being. Guests who encounter this scent in the hotel lobby associate it with comfort and luxury, enhancing the overall experience and deepening their emotional connection to the brand.

Touch: the feel of quality

The sense of touch can be a powerful tool in communicating a brand's values, particularly when it comes to quality. A well-crafted product that feels substantial, smooth, or luxurious in the hands can elevate a brand's image and influence customer perceptions. The materials used in packaging, the texture of a product, or even the physical environment of a store all contribute to how a brand is experienced.

Apple, for example, has mastered the use of touch in its product design. The smooth, cool feel of the iPhone or the precision and weight of the MacBook's aluminum casing give users a tactile sense of quality and craftsmanship. Apple's physical retail spaces are also designed to encourage touch, with open displays that invite customers to pick up and interact with the products. This tactile interaction enhances the overall brand experience, reinforcing Apple's identity as a brand that values innovation, quality, and sleek design.

Luxury brands like Hermès take this a step further. The feel of their leather goods is a crucial part of their appeal, as the softness and durability of the material communicate craftsmanship and exclusivity. When customers pick up a Hermès handbag, they're not just buying an accessory—they're experiencing the brand's heritage and dedication to quality through the sense of touch.

Sound: crafting an auditory identity

Sound is another critical component of sensory branding. From the music played in stores to the sound a product makes, auditory cues can evoke specific emotions and reinforce brand identity. Sound helps create a mood, set expectations, and enhance the overall experience of interacting with a brand.

Think of how McDonald's uses sound in its branding. The famous "I'm Lovin' It" jingle is instantly recognizable, acting as an auditory signature that ties together McDonald's advertising, in-store experience, and even drive-thru interactions. The jingle reinforces McDonald's brand personality of fun, lightheartedness, and universal appeal. Every time customers hear it, they are reminded of the brand's promise of joy and indulgence.

Automotive brands also rely heavily on sound to convey quality and performance. The sound of a car engine, for instance, plays a significant role in shaping perceptions of the brand. The deep, rumbling roar of a Harley-Davidson motorcycle is iconic, evoking feelings of freedom, power, and rebellion. Harley-Davidson has even gone so far as to trademark its engine sound, recognizing its importance in reinforcing the brand's image.

In retail environments, soundscapes can greatly influence customer behavior. Research shows that slower, more ambient music can encourage customers to spend more time in stores, while upbeat, fast-paced music can create a sense of energy and excitement. Brands like Starbucks carefully curate the music played in their cafes to match the mood of their spaces, reinforcing the brand's focus on creating a warm, relaxed environment for socializing or working.

Taste: memorable flavor experiences

For food and beverage brands, taste is obviously a central part of the customer experience, but sensory branding through taste can extend beyond just the product itself. Creating signature flavors or taste experiences can help differentiate a brand and foster loyalty.

Coca-Cola's distinct taste is one of the most recognizable in the world, with its secret recipe forming the foundation of its brand identity. The flavor of Coca-Cola isn't just a product feature — it's a sensory experience that evokes nostalgia, happiness, and refreshment. This signature taste is so deeply ingrained in the brand's identity that it has become part of Coca-Cola's global cultural footprint.

But taste isn't just limited to food and drink brands. Non-food companies have also begun experimenting with taste experiences to enhance their brand expression. For instance, high-end hotels like Ritz-Carlton often provide complimentary chocolates or flavored water in their lobbies, giving guests a taste that complements the luxury experience of staying at the hotel. This small gesture helps build a sensory connection with the brand, making the overall experience feel more indulgent and thoughtful.

Visuals: going beyond the logo

While sensory branding often emphasizes lesser-used senses like smell or touch, sight remains a crucial part of the equation. However, sensory branding through visuals goes beyond just logos and color schemes. It's about creating immersive environments and visual experiences that engage customers and reinforce the brand's values.

Brands like IKEA excel at visual branding, turning their stores into experiential spaces that invite customers to see their products in real-life settings. Each room display is carefully curated to show IKEA's products in a way that feels attainable and inspirational, making customers imagine how the products might look in their own homes. This visual storytelling not only highlights the functionality of the products but also reinforces IKEA's brand promise of affordability and practicality.

Similarly, beauty brand Lush uses bold, colorful displays in its stores to enhance the sensory experience. The sight of the vibrant, handmade products arranged in creative ways invites customers to touch, smell, and engage with them. The visual appeal of the products is integral to Lush's identity as a brand that values freshness, fun, and ethical sourcing.

Crafting a multi-sensory brand experience

Sensory branding is most effective when multiple senses are engaged simultaneously, creating a holistic brand experience. The more senses a brand can activate, the stronger the emotional connection it can build with its audience. Engaging multiple senses makes the brand experience feel richer, more immersive, and more memorable.

Brands that craft a multi-sensory experience can create deep emotional bonds with their customers. Think of Disney theme parks, where sight, sound, smell, and even taste come together to create a magical experience. From the iconic Cinderella Castle to the smells of popcorn and churros wafting through the air, every sense is carefully orchestrated to immerse visitors in the Disney brand. It's this multi-sensory approach that makes a trip to Disneyland feel like stepping into another world, leaving guests with lasting memories and a deep emotional attachment to the brand.

The power of sensory branding lies in its ability to go beyond what customers expect. By engaging more than just sight and sound, brands can create experiences that feel personal, memorable, and emotionally resonant. In an age where customers are bombarded with information, brands that engage multiple senses stand out—and leave a lasting impression.

Brand Experience vs. Customer Experience: where the two meet

In the world of branding and marketing, two terms often come up: brand experience and customer experience. While they might seem interchangeable, they represent different aspects of how people interact with a company. Understanding the distinction—and how the two overlap—is essential for brands that want to create lasting relationships with their audience.

Brand experience is about how a company expresses its identity and values through every touchpoint. It's the personality and emotion the brand evokes, from its messaging and design to how it presents itself in the marketplace. Customer experience, on the other hand, is about how individuals perceive their interactions with the brand. It's the personal journey a customer takes when they engage with a company's products, services, or people.

When done right, these two elements work together seamlessly, creating a powerful emotional connection that goes beyond a single transaction. Where brand experience sets the tone, customer experience is the journey. Together, they define how a customer feels about the brand, influencing loyalty, advocacy, and long-term success.

The brand experience: creating a cohesive identity

At its core, brand experience is about creating a cohesive identity that resonates with consumers. It's how a brand makes people feel, and it's shaped by every element of the brand's expression—from its logo and website design to its advertising and social media presence. Brand experience is the intentional effort a company makes to create an emotional connection with its audience, reinforcing its core values and personality across every touchpoint.

Think about Nike. The Nike brand experience isn't just about selling athletic shoes or gear. It's about inspiring individuals to push their limits and achieve greatness. From the bold, motivational language of their ads to the clean, empowering design of their website, Nike consistently delivers a brand experience that reflects its essence: empowerment, strength, and victory. Whether you're watching a Nike commercial or shopping at a Nike store, the feeling is the same—you're being encouraged to "Just Do It."

A strong brand experience gives customers a clear sense of who the brand is and what it stands for. This identity becomes the foundation for every interaction, setting expectations for what consumers will experience when they engage with the brand.

The customer experience: the journey of interaction

While brand experience sets the stage, customer experience is what happens when individuals actually engage with the brand. It's about the practical, day-to-day interactions people have with a company's products, services, or customer support. Customer experience encompasses everything from how easy it is to navigate a website to how friendly and responsive customer service is. It's the reality of dealing with a brand, and it's often the most immediate factor in shaping a customer's satisfaction—or dissatisfaction.

A good customer experience focuses on convenience, ease of use, and satisfaction. Amazon is a prime example of a company that has mastered customer experience. From one-click shopping to fast, reliable shipping, Amazon has streamlined every aspect of the customer journey to make it as frictionless as possible. Its return process is simple, customer support is easy to access, and the platform is optimized for quick, efficient transactions. Amazon's focus on removing barriers to purchase has made it one of the most successful e-commerce brands in the world.

While brand experience is largely about the emotional connection, customer experience is about practical efficiency and delivering on promises. A company can have an amazing brand identity, but if the customer's experience doesn't live up to expectations—if the website is difficult to use, the product doesn't arrive on time, or customer service is poor—the overall perception of the brand will suffer.

Where brand and customer experience meet

The magic happens where brand experience and customer experience intersect. While each serves a distinct function, the most successful companies are those that blend them seamlessly, creating an emotionally charged journey that also meets practical needs. When a brand's identity aligns with how customers experience the company, it strengthens loyalty and creates a sense of trust.

Take Apple as an example. Apple's brand experience is all about simplicity, innovation, and premium quality. This identity is reflected in its sleek product design, minimalist stores, and straightforward advertising. But Apple's customer experience is equally well-executed. From the intuitive layout of its website to the ease of using its products, every interaction feels effortless. Even customer service at the Apple Store or online is consistent with the brand's promise of simplicity and innovation. The brand experience sets high expectations, and the customer experience delivers on them.

When brand experience and customer experience are disconnected, however, it creates confusion and disappointment. Imagine a luxury brand that promises exclusivity and quality through its branding but provides poor customer service or delivers products that don't meet expectations. The disconnect between the brand's image and the customer's reality leads to frustration, eroding trust in the brand.

Creating synergy between brand and customer experience

For brands to build strong, lasting relationships with their customers, they need to ensure that their brand experience and customer experience are aligned. This requires clear communication across all levels of the business, from marketing to customer service to product development. Every team needs to understand the brand's core identity and how it should be reflected in the customer experience.

Consistency is key. Brands like Starbucks excel in this area, creating synergy between their brand experience and customer experience. Starbucks positions itself as a brand centered around comfort, community, and high-quality coffee. This promise is fulfilled in the customer experience: baristas are trained to be friendly and knowledgeable, the environment is warm and inviting, and the app makes ordering and paying seamless. The end result is that Starbucks feels the same whether you're browsing their Instagram or visiting a local store.

In today's competitive marketplace, aligning brand and customer experience requires brands to continually listen to their customers, adjust their processes, and stay true to their identity. It's not just about creating a visually appealing brand—it's about delivering on that promise in every interaction.

The emotional impact of alignment

When brand experience and customer experience are aligned, the emotional impact on the customer is profound. Customers feel more connected to the brand, not just because of what it offers but because of how it makes them feel. This emotional connection is what drives loyalty and turns customers into advocates.

Take Disney, a brand that excels in creating magical experiences. Disney's brand experience is built around the idea of wonder, joy, and nostalgia, and this identity is reflected in every touchpoint, from its movies and theme parks to its customer service and merchandise. The Disney experience feels seamless, whether you're interacting with the brand online, at a theme park, or through a streaming service like Disney+. Customers don't just visit Disney—they feel part of the Disney magic, creating an emotional bond that keeps them coming back.

This emotional connection is what sets apart brands that are merely transactional from those that are beloved. When a brand's experience matches the customer's experience, the result is trust, loyalty, and an enduring relationship.

CHAPTER 05
THE FIFTH E

Engagement

The customer journey: Mapping engagement from awareness to advocacy

A customer's relationship with a brand doesn't begin and end with a single purchase. The journey a customer takes—from the moment they first hear about a brand to the point where they become a loyal advocate—is long, multifaceted, and often nonlinear. For brands, mapping this journey is key to understanding how to engage customers at every touchpoint. By identifying where customers are in their journey and meeting their needs at each stage, brands can foster deeper connections, drive conversions, and build long-lasting loyalty.

A well-crafted customer journey maps out the critical moments where a customer interacts with a brand, from initial awareness to eventual advocacy. By breaking down these stages, brands can create targeted strategies to nurture engagement, ensuring that each touchpoint enhances the customer's experience and brings them closer to becoming a brand advocate.

Stage 1: Awareness—introducing the brand

The customer journey begins with awareness. At this stage, potential customers are discovering your brand for the first time. They may not yet know what your brand offers, but something has sparked their interest—a social media ad, a word-of-mouth recommendation, or even a product placement. The goal at this stage is to make a memorable first impression and start building familiarity.

For many brands, awareness is about visibility. Social media, online advertising, influencer partnerships, and SEO strategies all play a key role in getting the brand in front of new audiences. However, simply being visible isn't enough—brands need to communicate their value proposition quickly and clearly. This means creating engaging content that resonates with the target audience's needs, values, and lifestyle.

For example, Spotify's early campaigns focused on creating awareness by highlighting the freedom of on-demand music streaming. Their "Music for everyone" slogan and personalized playlists appealed to a wide audience, making Spotify instantly memorable. By focusing on what made them different from traditional music services, they were able to capture attention and generate interest from first-time listeners.

At this stage, customers are gathering information and comparing brands, so it's important for brands to focus on creating content that educates and entices, making it clear what sets them apart from competitors.

Stage 2: Consideration—building trust and credibility

Once a customer is aware of your brand, they enter the consideration stage. Here, they're doing more research, looking at reviews, and comparing options to see which brand fits their needs best. This is where trust and credibility become crucial. Customers want to know that your brand is reliable, and they need proof that you can deliver on your promises.

To build trust during this stage, brands need to provide social proof — whether through customer reviews, testimonials, case studies, or influencer endorsements. User-generated content is especially powerful at this stage, as it shows real customers having positive experiences with the brand. Providing transparent information about the product or service also helps reassure potential customers that they are making a well-informed decision.

Glossier, the beauty brand, excels at the consideration stage by leveraging its community of users to build trust. Glossier encourages customers to share their beauty routines and product experiences, creating a wealth of authentic reviews and testimonials. By showcasing real people using their products, Glossier builds credibility and helps potential customers see themselves as part of the brand's community.

Content marketing also plays a key role in this phase. Educational blog posts, tutorials, videos, and product comparisons help customers understand the value of your brand and make informed choices. Brands should focus on answering common customer questions and addressing pain points to position themselves as trusted advisors in their field.

Stage 3: Decision — driving conversion

Once a customer has done their research and narrowed down their options, they enter the decision stage. This is the moment when they decide whether or not to purchase from your brand. At this point, the customer needs a final push — something that convinces them that your brand is the right choice.

Incentives like free trials, discounts, or limited-time offers can help drive conversions by giving potential customers a reason to act now. Brands should also streamline the purchase process, making it as easy and frictionless as possible. A complicated checkout experience can turn customers away, while a smooth, intuitive process increases the likelihood of conversion.

Apple is known for simplifying the decision stage through its clean, easy-to-navigate website and seamless checkout process. Apple's design not only makes it easy to browse products but also highlights key features and benefits at just the right moments. Coupled with Apple's strong brand identity and customer trust, these factors make it easier for customers to move from consideration to purchase.

At this stage, it's important to remove any remaining barriers to purchase. Offering multiple payment options, clear return policies, and responsive customer support can all help reduce hesitation and encourage customers to complete their purchase.

Stage 4: Retention—nurturing loyalty

Once a customer has made a purchase, the journey doesn't end—this is where retention comes into play. The goal at this stage is to nurture customer loyalty by creating a positive post-purchase experience that keeps them coming back. This means delivering on your promises, offering excellent customer service, and staying engaged with the customer beyond the transaction.

For many brands, the post-purchase experience is where they have the opportunity to shine. Personalized follow-up emails, onboarding support, and loyalty programs all help ensure that customers feel valued and appreciated. Brands that invest in building relationships with their customers after the sale are more likely to see repeat purchases and increased brand loyalty.

Amazon's Prime membership is a great example of how brands can use retention strategies to keep customers engaged. By offering free shipping, exclusive deals, and streaming services, Amazon creates added value for its customers, encouraging them to stay loyal to the brand. These perks, combined with Amazon's user-friendly shopping experience, turn first-time buyers into long-term customers.

At the retention stage, brands should focus on staying top of mind through regular communication, personalized offers, and ongoing support. By making customers feel like they're part of a community or offering exclusive benefits, brands can turn one-time buyers into repeat customers.

Stage 5: Advocacy—turning customers into ambassadors

The final stage of the customer journey is advocacy. At this point, a customer has had such a positive experience with your brand that they become a brand advocate, sharing their love for your products or services with others. These advocates are often willing to promote your brand through word-of-mouth, social media, and even reviews, helping you reach new customers organically.

To foster advocacy, brands need to make it easy for customers to share their experiences. Encouraging user-generated content, offering referral programs, or creating social media challenges can all help turn satisfied customers into brand advocates. The key is to reward and recognize these customers for their loyalty, making them feel valued and appreciated for their contributions.

Tesla's referral program is a prime example of how to create advocates out of loyal customers. Tesla owners are rewarded for referring new buyers to the brand, offering perks like free Supercharging miles and exclusive invitations to events. This not only incentivizes advocacy but also strengthens the bond between Tesla and its loyal customer base.

Brands should also focus on maintaining open lines of communication with their most loyal customers, seeking feedback and involving them in product development or exclusive events. By fostering a sense of community and inclusion, brands can turn customers into passionate advocates who promote the brand on their own.

Creating a seamless journey: connecting the dots

While each stage of the customer journey has its own challenges, the most successful brands are those that create a seamless, connected experience from awareness to advocacy. This means ensuring that every touchpoint feels consistent, aligned with the brand's identity, and responsive to the customer's needs.

A great customer journey doesn't just happen—it's carefully crafted. Brands need to anticipate potential pain points and provide solutions at each stage, guiding customers smoothly from one phase to the next. By doing so, brands can create an experience that not only satisfies but delights, turning casual customers into lifelong advocates.

Customer service as brand engagement: Turning complaints into opportunities.

Customer service is often seen as a way to resolve problems, but it's much more than that. It's a critical touchpoint that can shape how customers perceive your brand, and it presents a unique opportunity to turn a potentially negative interaction—like a complaint—into a positive one. When handled effectively, customer service becomes a powerful tool for building engagement, fostering loyalty, and even turning dissatisfied customers into brand advocates.

At its core, customer service is about delivering on a brand's promise, ensuring that every interaction reflects the brand's values and commitment to customer satisfaction. Brands that approach customer service as an opportunity for engagement rather than just a problem-solving mechanism can create deeper connections with their customers, strengthen trust, and enhance the overall customer experience.

The importance of proactive customer service

In the digital age, where customers expect immediate responses and personalized solutions, customer service is more than just answering questions—it's about anticipating needs and proactively addressing concerns. Proactive customer service means reaching out to customers before issues arise or escalating problems are avoided. This not only reduces the likelihood of complaints but also makes customers feel valued and cared for.

Brands like Zappos have built their reputation on exceptional customer service by going above and beyond what's expected. Zappos' customer service team is known for taking the time to connect with customers on a personal level, even if it means long phone calls to resolve minor issues. This proactive approach creates memorable interactions that make customers feel heard, understood, and appreciated. By focusing on building relationships rather than just solving problems, Zappos has turned customer service into a key differentiator that drives loyalty and engagement.

When brands are proactive, they send a clear message: we care about you, not just when there's a problem, but throughout your entire journey with us. This type of engagement can prevent small issues from becoming big complaints and reinforces the brand's commitment to customer satisfaction.

Turning complaints into loyalty-building moments

Complaints are inevitable, but how a brand handles them can make all the difference. Every complaint is an opportunity to not only resolve an issue but to demonstrate the brand's integrity, responsiveness, and care for its customers. When handled with empathy and efficiency, complaints can become loyalty-building moments, transforming an unhappy customer into a loyal one.

Take Apple, for example. Apple's Genius Bar, both in-store and online, is a cornerstone of the brand's customer service strategy. Customers who experience issues with their devices are guided through a personalized, hands-on support process that focuses on solving their problem in a way that feels attentive and thorough. Whether it's a hardware repair, a software issue, or even just user error, Apple's commitment to high-touch customer service leaves customers feeling reassured and more likely to remain loyal, even after a problem.

When brands handle complaints poorly, they risk losing customers—and worse, those dissatisfied customers may share their negative experiences online, damaging the brand's reputation. But when brands respond to complaints quickly, take responsibility, and offer meaningful solutions, they can turn a negative experience into a positive one, leaving the customer feeling valued and appreciated.

The role of empathy in customer service

One of the most important elements of effective customer service is empathy. Customers want to feel understood, especially when they're upset or frustrated. By showing genuine empathy and taking the time to listen to their concerns, brands can de-escalate tense situations and build trust.

Southwest Airlines is a great example of a brand that uses empathy as a cornerstone of its customer service strategy. When passengers face flight delays, cancellations, or other disruptions, Southwest's customer service team is trained to respond with understanding and a willingness to make things right. Whether through proactive communication, personalized assistance, or compensatory gestures, the airline demonstrates empathy in every interaction, often going out of its way to make sure customers leave with a positive impression, even after a negative situation.

Empathy is more than just saying the right words—it's about actively listening to the customer's concerns and addressing them with care and respect. When brands approach customer service with empathy, they create a human connection that goes beyond the transaction, fostering long-term loyalty.

Personalizing the customer service experience

In today's world, customers expect personalized experiences, and customer service is no exception. Generic responses and one-size-fits-all solutions can leave customers feeling unimportant. On the other hand, personalized customer service—tailored to each individual's needs and preferences—can make customers feel valued and seen, enhancing their overall experience with the brand.

Amazon has perfected the art of personalized customer service. Through its data-driven approach, Amazon can quickly access a customer's order history, track interactions, and provide tailored support based on previous purchases and experiences. This personalization allows Amazon to resolve issues more efficiently while making the customer feel like they are receiving individualized attention.

Personalizing customer service doesn't just mean addressing customers by their names—it means understanding their unique challenges and offering solutions that are relevant to their specific situation. Whether it's offering a replacement, suggesting alternatives based on past behavior, or simply acknowledging their loyalty, personalization builds a stronger bond between the customer and the brand.

Leveraging technology to enhance customer service

Technology has transformed the way brands deliver customer service, making it faster, more accessible, and often more efficient. With the rise of chatbots, AI-driven support, and automated systems, brands can provide instant responses and resolve common issues quickly. However, while technology can enhance customer service, it's important to strike the right balance between automation and human interaction.

Chatbots, for example, are excellent for handling simple inquiries, like order tracking or FAQs, freeing up human agents to focus on more complex problems. Brands like H&M use chatbots on their website and social media platforms to handle routine questions, providing customers with quick answers 24/7. But when a customer has a more personalized or nuanced issue, H&M ensures that they can easily connect with a human agent, allowing for a more thoughtful and empathetic response.

By integrating technology into customer service in a way that enhances, rather than replaces, human interaction, brands can offer faster, more efficient support while still maintaining a personal touch.

Turning customer feedback into actionable insights

Customer service is also one of the most valuable sources of feedback. Complaints, questions, and suggestions provide brands with critical insights into customer needs, pain points, and areas for improvement. Brands that actively listen to their customers and use this feedback to improve their products, services, or processes can stay ahead of the curve and continuously refine the customer experience.

Brands like Netflix have successfully used customer feedback to enhance their service. By closely monitoring customer concerns, Netflix has made numerous improvements to its platform, from adding new features like "Skip Intro" to refining its recommendation algorithm. Each update is a response to customer input, demonstrating that Netflix listens and acts on feedback.

Collecting and analyzing customer feedback helps brands identify patterns and trends that can inform future decisions, from product development to marketing strategies. Brands that make it clear they are listening to their customers create a sense of collaboration, making customers feel valued as active participants in the brand's evolution.

The long-term value of excellent customer service

Excellent customer service isn't just about resolving issues—it's about creating positive, memorable interactions that keep customers coming back. In fact, studies show that customers are more likely to remain loyal to a brand after a positive customer service experience, even if there was a problem initially. By turning complaints into opportunities for engagement, brands can build lasting loyalty and advocacy.

Nordstrom, known for its exceptional customer service, has built a reputation for going above and beyond for its customers. From no-questions-asked returns to personalized shopping experiences, Nordstrom's commitment to service has earned the brand a loyal following. Customers who have positive service experiences are more likely to share their stories, whether through word-of-mouth or online reviews, amplifying the brand's reputation for excellence.

At the end of the day, customer service is one of the most direct ways a brand can show it values its customers. By handling complaints with empathy, personalizing responses, and leveraging technology, brands can turn customer service into a strategic tool for engagement, turning everyday interactions into moments of connection and loyalty.

Community building: how engagement turns customers into brand advocates

In today's world, successful brands are more than just products or services—they are communities. Building a strong brand community not only deepens engagement with customers but also transforms them into passionate advocates. When customers feel connected to a brand's values, mission, and community, they are more likely to engage, spread the word, and advocate for the brand organically. This sense of belonging turns a simple purchase into an ongoing relationship, where customers don't just buy—they contribute, support, and amplify the brand's message.

A well-crafted community framework fosters trust, loyalty, and shared identity, turning casual customers into advocates who help grow the brand through authentic, word-of-mouth recommendations. The best communities give customers a space to connect with each other, share experiences, and feel like they are part of something larger than a simple transaction.

Why community matters: creating a sense of belonging

At the heart of every successful brand community is a sense of belonging. People want to feel part of something that reflects their values, lifestyle, and aspirations. By building a community around shared beliefs or goals, brands can create a deeper emotional connection with their audience, making customers feel more engaged and invested in the brand's journey.

Take Harley-Davidson as an example. The Harley Owners Group (H.O.G.) is one of the most well-known brand communities, built around the shared passion of motorcycle enthusiasts. Members of H.O.G. don't just ride Harley bikes—they're part of a lifestyle. Harley-Davidson has cultivated a community that thrives on a sense of brotherhood, adventure, and freedom. By organizing events, rides, and social gatherings, the brand has built a network of loyal customers who proudly advocate for the brand, turning their personal experiences into a powerful form of word-of-mouth marketing.

For brands, fostering this kind of belonging means creating spaces where customers can connect with each other as much as they connect with the brand. When people feel like they are part of a community, they are more likely to become advocates, sharing their positive experiences and encouraging others to join.

Engagement through shared values

A strong community thrives on shared values. Brands that clearly articulate their mission and beliefs attract customers who align with those values. When customers see themselves reflected in a brand's message, they feel a deeper connection, making them more likely to engage and advocate for the brand.

Take Patagonia, for instance. The outdoor clothing company has built a community around its commitment to environmental sustainability. Patagonia's community members are not just customers—they are advocates for environmental activism. The brand actively involves its community in initiatives like environmental campaigns, recycling programs, and conservation efforts. By aligning with values that matter to its customers, Patagonia transforms those customers into advocates who see their purchase as part of a greater cause.

By focusing on shared values, brands create a community where members feel empowered to act, whether it's through purchasing decisions, participation in brand-driven events, or spreading the word about the brand's mission.

Encouraging user-generated content

One of the most effective ways to turn customers into brand advocates is by encouraging them to create and share content. User-generated content (UGC) is a powerful tool because it allows customers to become active participants in the brand's story. When customers share photos, videos, or reviews, they aren't just engaging with the brand—they're advocating for it in a personal, authentic way.

Glossier is a beauty brand that has excelled at fostering UGC within its community. The brand actively encourages its customers to share their skincare routines, product experiences, and beauty tips on social media. Glossier then amplifies this content by featuring it on their website and social platforms. This creates a loop of engagement where customers feel valued for their contributions and see themselves as part of the brand's identity.

By empowering customers to become content creators, brands can generate organic buzz and build credibility. UGC doesn't just promote the brand; it builds trust, as potential customers are more likely to trust the opinions and experiences of real people over traditional marketing campaigns.

Building engagement through exclusivity

Exclusivity is a key driver of engagement within brand communities. When customers feel like they have access to something unique, they are more likely to become loyal advocates. Brands that offer exclusive content, products, or experiences create a sense of special belonging, making customers feel like insiders.

Supreme is a brand that has mastered the art of exclusivity. By releasing limited-edition "drops," Supreme creates a sense of urgency and scarcity that drives customer engagement. Fans of the brand eagerly await each new release, knowing that only a select few will be able to get their hands on the products. This exclusivity fuels excitement and loyalty, with customers proudly promoting the brand as part of a rare, coveted community.

Exclusivity doesn't have to be product-based. Brands can offer exclusive access to events, early releases, or behind-the-scenes content to make customers feel like valued insiders. These experiences create stronger emotional bonds and make customers more likely to share their enthusiasm with others.

Rewarding loyalty and advocacy

A brand community thrives when its members feel appreciated for their loyalty and contributions. Recognizing and rewarding advocates for their engagement not only strengthens their connection to the brand but also encourages others to become more active participants.

Brands like Sephora have built loyalty programs that go beyond discounts and rewards. Sephora's *Beauty Insider* program not only offers points for purchases but also includes personalized product recommendations, exclusive event invitations, and early access to new products. By offering perks that feel tailored to the individual, Sephora creates a community where members feel valued and are incentivized to keep advocating for the brand.

Publicly acknowledging advocates can also amplify engagement. Brands like Lululemon highlight their most loyal customers on social media, showcasing their stories, fitness journeys, and brand love. This recognition not only makes those individuals feel special but also inspires others in the community to engage more actively in the hopes of being recognized.

Turning community into advocacy

The ultimate goal of building a brand community is to create advocates who are passionate about spreading the word. This happens when customers feel like they are part of something meaningful—whether it's a lifestyle, a movement, or a group of like-minded individuals who share common goals. When customers identify with a brand's community, they are more likely to tell others about it, leading to organic growth driven by trust and authenticity.

Nike's *Nike Run Club* is a perfect example of a community that fosters advocacy. The brand has created a global network of runners who connect through local running groups, share their progress on the app, and participate in challenges. These runners don't just use Nike products—they are actively promoting the Nike brand through their shared experiences. The sense of camaraderie and support within the Nike Run Club encourages members to invite others to join, spreading the brand's message of empowerment and achievement.

By creating a space where customers can connect with each other, brands can harness the power of community to drive advocacy. When customers feel a sense of ownership and pride in the brand, they naturally become its most vocal supporters.

Customer retention strategies: keeping your community engaged

Retaining customers is just as important as acquiring them. In fact, it's often more cost-effective to keep existing customers engaged than to constantly find new ones. Customer retention is about fostering long-term relationships that go beyond a single transaction and creating a community where customers feel valued and connected to the brand. Engaging with your community consistently and meaningfully is key to ensuring customers stay loyal and continue to advocate for your brand.

Effective customer retention strategies focus on maintaining engagement, rewarding loyalty, and building a sense of belonging. When customers feel like they are part of a community, they are more likely to stick around, share their experiences, and remain active participants in the brand's journey.

Why retention matters: loyalty drives growth

Loyal customers don't just come back—they tend to spend more, buy more often, and are more likely to recommend the brand to others. Research shows that increasing customer retention by as little as 5% can increase profits by up to 95%. The reason? Loyal customers already trust your brand, so they're less likely to be swayed by competitors and more likely to explore new offerings from your company.

Retention strategies help create a sustainable growth model. Instead of constantly pouring resources into new customer acquisition, brands that focus on retention can build lasting relationships that drive long-term profitability. These relationships also create a network of advocates who can amplify the brand's message organically.

Personalization: creating individualized experiences

Personalization is one of the most effective ways to keep customers engaged. Customers today expect personalized experiences that cater to their preferences, behavior, and needs. By tailoring interactions, recommendations, and communications, brands can make customers feel valued and understood.

Amazon excels at personalization by using data to deliver tailored product recommendations, personalized emails, and a customized shopping experience. From suggesting products based on past purchases to reminding customers about items they've browsed, Amazon creates a shopping environment that feels unique to each individual. This level of personalization keeps customers coming back because they feel that the brand understands their preferences.

Brands can leverage personalization through various touchpoints—whether it's through personalized marketing emails, product recommendations based on previous purchases, or loyalty programs that offer tailored rewards. The key is to make each customer feel like their experience is curated just for them, building a deeper connection that encourages them to stay engaged.

Loyalty programs: rewarding repeat customers

Loyalty programs are a tried-and-true method of keeping customers engaged. By rewarding repeat purchases and encouraging ongoing interaction, brands can create a sense of appreciation and incentivize long-term loyalty. The most effective loyalty programs go beyond points and discounts—they offer unique perks, exclusive access, and personalized rewards that make customers feel special.

Starbucks has built one of the most successful loyalty programs with its *Starbucks Rewards* app. Customers earn stars with every purchase, which they can redeem for free drinks, food, or other rewards. But the program goes further, offering personalized deals, birthday rewards, and early access to seasonal items. By rewarding repeat visits and creating a sense of exclusivity, Starbucks keeps its customers coming back for more.

Loyalty programs don't just drive repeat purchases—they also create a sense of achievement and exclusivity. When customers feel like they're part of an exclusive group with access to special perks, they are more likely to stay engaged with the brand.

Ongoing communication: staying top of mind

To keep customers engaged, brands need to stay in touch with them through regular, meaningful communication. Whether it's through email newsletters, social media updates, or mobile notifications, ongoing communication ensures that your brand remains top of mind. However, it's important that these communications provide value rather than simply promoting products.

Brands like Sephora use email newsletters to offer personalized beauty tips, exclusive deals, and early access to new products. Rather than bombarding customers with sales messages, Sephora focuses on delivering content that aligns with the interests of its audience. This approach not only keeps customers engaged but also reinforces Sephora's role as a trusted advisor in the beauty space.

Ongoing communication should focus on offering value, whether that's through educational content, personalized recommendations, or exclusive offers. By maintaining a regular presence in your customers' lives, you can build stronger connections and encourage ongoing engagement.

Building community: fostering connections

One of the most effective customer retention strategies is creating a sense of community. When customers feel like they are part of a community, they are more likely to remain loyal to the brand and engage with it over the long term. Building community means creating spaces where customers can connect with each other, share experiences, and feel a sense of belonging.

Nike has built a strong community around its *Nike Run Club*, which offers customers a platform to track their runs, share their progress, and connect with other runners. By creating challenges and offering virtual running events, Nike keeps its community engaged and motivated. This sense of shared purpose strengthens the bond between the brand and its customers, transforming runners into loyal advocates.

For brands, fostering a community can take many forms—from social media groups and forums to loyalty program communities or exclusive events. The goal is to create spaces where customers feel connected not only to the brand but also to each other, building a network of engaged, loyal followers.

Gathering feedback: showing customers you care

Listening to your customers is one of the best ways to show them that you value their opinions and are committed to improving their experience. Brands that actively seek feedback from their customers and use it to make meaningful changes demonstrate that they care about the customer journey. This kind of engagement fosters trust and encourages customers to stay loyal to the brand.

Brands like Netflix regularly gather feedback from their users to refine their content recommendations, improve their platform, and offer a better viewing experience. By incorporating customer feedback into its decision-making process, Netflix demonstrates that it is constantly working to improve and cater to the needs of its users.

Whether through surveys, product reviews, or direct interactions, brands that gather and act on customer feedback show that they are invested in creating the best possible experience for their customers. This builds trust and strengthens the relationship, encouraging long-term loyalty.

Surprise and delight: exceeding expectations

One of the most powerful ways to retain customers is by exceeding their expectations. This doesn't have to involve grand gestures—sometimes, small surprises can leave a lasting impression. Brands that go the extra mile to "surprise and delight" their customers create memorable experiences that keep them engaged and coming back for more.

For instance, Zappos is known for its exceptional customer service and often goes above and beyond to surprise its customers. Zappos might offer free overnight shipping or upgrade a customer's order unexpectedly, creating a positive, memorable experience. These small acts of kindness foster loyalty by making customers feel valued and appreciated.

"Surprise and delight" strategies can take many forms—from unexpected gifts or personalized thank-you notes to exclusive offers or upgrades. The goal is to create moments that stand out, leaving customers with a positive impression that strengthens their bond with the brand.

Measuring retention: understanding what works

To successfully retain customers, brands need to track and measure retention metrics. This includes monitoring customer churn, repeat purchase rates, customer lifetime value, and engagement rates across different touchpoints. By analyzing these metrics, brands can identify what's working, where customers are falling off, and how to refine their retention strategies.

Tools like customer relationship management (CRM) systems and analytics platforms allow brands to track customer behavior and engagement, providing valuable insights into how to improve the customer experience. Regularly reviewing these metrics helps brands make informed decisions that keep customers engaged and loyal over the long term.

Creating a brand community framework: from loyal customers to brand ambassadors

Loyal customers are the backbone of any successful brand, but the true power of loyalty lies in turning those customers into brand ambassadors. A brand community framework is a powerful way to cultivate this transformation. By building a community around shared values, interests, and experiences, brands can create a network of customers who not only purchase their products but also passionately advocate for them.

Brand ambassadors are more than just repeat buyers; they're customers who feel a deep connection to your brand and actively share that connection with others. Whether through word-of-mouth, social media, or personal recommendations, brand ambassadors help spread your message, drive organic growth, and reinforce brand loyalty in ways traditional advertising can't.

But creating a brand community isn't just about creating a fan club — it's about fostering genuine relationships, building trust, and delivering consistent value. This requires intentional effort from brands to engage, support, and empower their community members, transforming them from loyal customers into active advocates.

The foundation of a brand community: shared values and purpose

At the heart of every strong brand community is a shared sense of purpose. People are more likely to join a community when they feel connected to a cause, value, or identity that aligns with their own beliefs. This shared purpose gives customers a reason to engage with the brand beyond the product or service itself, creating a sense of belonging and identity within the community.

Take Patagonia, for example. The brand has built a community of environmentally conscious consumers who share its values around sustainability and environmental activism. Patagonia's dedication to environmental causes isn't just marketing; it's a core part of the brand's identity. By supporting initiatives like climate action, recycling programs, and ethical sourcing, Patagonia gives its customers a reason to believe in the brand and rally around its mission. Customers don't just buy Patagonia products — they become part of a movement, feeling empowered to contribute to causes they care about. This alignment between brand values and customer beliefs turns buyers into advocates who passionately support the brand's mission and encourage others to join.

Fostering engagement through authentic connection

Creating a thriving brand community isn't just about gathering like-minded customers—it's about fostering genuine relationships and encouraging two-way engagement. The most successful brand communities are those where customers feel heard, valued, and appreciated. Brands that actively engage with their community members, respond to their feedback, and involve them in brand decisions create a sense of ownership among their customers, making them feel like an integral part of the brand's journey.

Glossier is a prime example of a brand that has mastered community engagement. The beauty brand built its community by actively listening to its customers on social media, taking their feedback into account when developing new products, and creating content that reflects the real experiences of its users. Glossier encourages its community members to share their beauty routines and product reviews, fostering a culture of authenticity and trust. By creating a space where customers can interact not only with the brand but with each other, Glossier has turned its community into a loyal, engaged group of brand ambassadors who proudly spread the word about their products.

Brands that take the time to engage meaningfully with their community create more than just brand loyalty—they create brand advocates who feel personally invested in the brand's success.

Empowering customers to share their stories

One of the most effective ways to turn loyal customers into brand ambassadors is by empowering them to share their own stories. User-generated content (UGC) has become a powerful tool for building brand communities because it gives customers a voice, allowing them to express their personal connection to the brand. When customers share their experiences, whether through photos, reviews, or social media posts, they humanize the brand and create authentic touchpoints for potential new customers.

Brands like Airbnb have successfully used UGC to build a vibrant community of hosts and travelers. By encouraging users to share stories of their unique stays and experiences, Airbnb has turned its customers into storytellers who actively promote the brand. These personal stories, shared through social media and the Airbnb website, create a sense of community while highlighting the diversity and authenticity of Airbnb's offerings. The brand's focus on celebrating its users, rather than simply promoting its own services, reinforces the idea that Airbnb is about shared experiences and belonging.

Encouraging customers to share their stories also taps into the powerful influence of social proof. Potential customers are more likely to trust recommendations and experiences shared by their peers than by the brand itself, making UGC a highly effective strategy for building credibility and trust within the community.

Recognizing and rewarding brand advocates

Recognition and rewards play a critical role in transforming loyal customers into active brand ambassadors. People want to feel valued for their loyalty, and when brands go out of their way to acknowledge and reward their most engaged customers, it deepens the emotional connection. Whether through exclusive offers, VIP access, or public recognition, brands that reward their advocates strengthen their relationship with their community.

Lululemon, for instance, has built a community around fitness and wellness, actively engaging its most loyal customers by offering them exclusive opportunities. The brand's *Sweat Collective* program invites fitness professionals and athletes to join a select group of influencers who receive discounts on Lululemon products, early access to new releases, and invitations to special events. This sense of exclusivity and recognition makes these advocates feel like they are an important part of the brand's ecosystem, further incentivizing them to promote Lululemon within their own networks.

Public recognition is another effective way to reward brand advocates. Brands like Sephora regularly highlight their most active community members on social media or within their online forums, giving them a platform to share their beauty tips, reviews, or personal journeys. This recognition not only validates the advocate's contributions but also encourages others in the community to engage more actively in the hopes of being recognized as well.

Building a sense of exclusivity

Part of what turns customers into brand ambassadors is a feeling of belonging to an exclusive group. Creating a sense of exclusivity within a brand community makes customers feel special and valued, giving them a reason to stay engaged and loyal. This exclusivity doesn't necessarily have to come from high price points or limited availability—it can be created through access to special content, events, or experiences that aren't available to the general public.

Brands like Supreme have leveraged exclusivity as a core part of their community-building strategy. Supreme's limited-edition product drops, known as "drops," create a sense of urgency and exclusivity that drives demand and encourages customers to become part of a select group of buyers. Fans of the brand become brand ambassadors, not just because they love the products but because they are proud to be part of an exclusive community with access to something rare and highly coveted.

Exclusivity can also come in the form of loyalty programs, private events, or insider access. By offering something unique and limited to their most loyal customers, brands can create a sense of belonging that motivates customers to continue engaging and advocating for the brand.

Creating opportunities for advocacy

The final step in turning loyal customers into brand ambassadors is providing them with opportunities to advocate for the brand. Whether through referral programs, social media campaigns, or ambassador programs, brands that make it easy for customers to share their love for the brand empower them to become active promoters.

Tesla, for example, has successfully used a referral program to incentivize its customers to spread the word about their vehicles. Tesla owners can refer friends and family to purchase Tesla vehicles, earning rewards like free Supercharging miles or exclusive invitations to Tesla events. This program not only rewards loyal customers but also turns them into advocates who actively promote the brand to their networks.

Social media challenges and campaigns can also be a powerful way to encourage advocacy. Brands like Red Bull regularly run challenges that invite customers to share videos of themselves taking on extreme sports or other adrenaline-pumping activities. These campaigns not only create a sense of excitement and community but also turn customers into active content creators who promote Red Bull through their personal stories.

The long-term value of brand ambassadors

Turning loyal customers into brand ambassadors is about more than just driving short-term sales—it's about building a sustainable, long-term relationship that adds value to both the brand and the customer. Brand ambassadors don't just promote the brand—they help shape its identity, contribute to its growth, and create a sense of belonging for others who share their values.

A strong brand community transforms customers from passive consumers into active participants in the brand's journey. By creating a framework that fosters engagement, celebrates loyalty, and empowers advocacy, brands can build a powerful network of ambassadors who amplify their message and drive organic growth.

CHAPTER 06
THE SIXTH E

Evolution

Brand building strategies: ensuring sustained growth over time

Building a successful brand is not just about gaining attention in the short term—it's about creating long-term growth and sustainability. As markets evolve, customer preferences shift, and new competitors emerge, brands must continually adapt and refine their strategies to stay relevant. Brand building is an ongoing process that requires consistent effort, innovation, and a clear vision for the future.

Sustained growth doesn't happen by chance; it's the result of thoughtful planning, strategic evolution, and a deep understanding of both the market and the customer. Brands that succeed over the long term are those that can evolve while staying true to their core identity, ensuring they remain relevant to their audience without losing what makes them unique.

Understanding the brand lifecycle

Every brand goes through a lifecycle—launch, growth, maturity, and, eventually, renewal or decline. To ensure sustained growth, it's essential to understand where your brand is in this lifecycle and adjust your strategies accordingly. Brands in the early stages of growth may focus on awareness and customer acquisition, while mature brands need to focus on innovation and diversification to stay relevant.

For example, Nike, a brand that has been around for decades, continues to evolve by expanding into new markets and categories. While it began as a running shoe company, Nike has successfully diversified into sportswear, fitness technology, and even content creation, positioning itself as a lifestyle brand. This ability to evolve while staying true to its core mission of inspiring athletes has allowed Nike to remain a market leader even as new competitors have emerged.

Brands that recognize their place in the lifecycle can make informed decisions about when to invest in growth, when to innovate, and when to rebrand or pivot to remain competitive. A clear understanding of the brand lifecycle allows for proactive planning rather than reactive strategies.

The importance of brand equity

Brand equity is the value that your brand holds in the minds of consumers. It's the result of years of consistent messaging, strong customer experiences, and a clear, differentiated identity. Brands with strong equity enjoy customer loyalty, are less price-sensitive, and can withstand market fluctuations better than those with weak brand equity.

Apple is a prime example of a brand with immense equity. Even though Apple's products often come at a premium price, its loyal customer base continues to purchase the latest devices because of the trust, innovation, and experience the brand delivers. Apple's equity allows it to maintain its position as a premium brand while constantly growing and evolving through new product lines and technology advancements.

Building and maintaining brand equity requires consistent messaging and delivering on your brand's promises. Every interaction a customer has with your brand—whether it's a product experience, a customer service interaction, or an ad campaign—contributes to building or eroding that equity. Brands that focus on delivering value and consistently meeting or exceeding customer expectations build the kind of loyalty that drives long-term growth.

Diversification: expanding your brand's reach

One of the most effective strategies for ensuring sustained growth is diversification. Brands that rely too heavily on a single product, market, or demographic risk stagnation as markets evolve. Diversifying your product offerings or expanding into new markets can help spread risk, tap into new customer segments, and drive growth over time.

Take Amazon as an example. What started as an online bookstore has expanded into a global marketplace, a cloud computing powerhouse, a streaming service, and a device manufacturer. Amazon's ability to diversify has allowed it to become a dominant player in multiple industries, ensuring continued growth even as the retail landscape has changed dramatically. By constantly exploring new opportunities and innovating, Amazon has evolved from an e-commerce giant into an all-encompassing tech leader.

For brands looking to diversify, it's essential to ensure that new products or markets align with the core identity and values of the brand. Expanding too far outside of the brand's perceived expertise can lead to confusion and dilute the brand's message. Successful diversification builds on the brand's strengths while exploring new opportunities that resonate with its existing customer base.

Innovation: staying ahead of market trends

In today's fast-paced business environment, innovation is crucial to long-term success. Brands that remain stagnant, relying solely on past successes, risk becoming irrelevant as new competitors emerge and customer preferences change. Innovation keeps brands fresh, exciting, and relevant, ensuring that they continue to meet the evolving needs of their audience.

Tesla is a brand that has made innovation a core part of its identity. From electric vehicles to solar energy solutions and autonomous driving technology, Tesla continually pushes the boundaries of what's possible in its industry. This commitment to innovation has allowed Tesla to disrupt the automotive market and build a brand that stands for forward-thinking, sustainable technology.

Innovation doesn't always have to be groundbreaking—it can also come in the form of incremental improvements that enhance the customer experience. Whether it's improving product functionality, offering new services, or finding more sustainable ways to produce goods, brands that consistently innovate are better positioned to adapt to market changes and maintain their growth trajectory.

Customer-centric strategies: keeping the customer at the heart of your evolution

While innovation and diversification are key to sustained growth, brands must never lose sight of their customers. A customer-centric approach ensures that as your brand evolves, it continues to meet the needs, preferences, and expectations of the people who matter most: your audience. Brands that focus on understanding and responding to their customers' evolving desires are more likely to maintain loyalty and grow over time.

Customer-centric strategies involve active listening—gathering feedback, monitoring trends, and staying engaged with your audience across multiple touchpoints. By understanding customer pain points and desires, brands can create products and experiences that resonate with their audience, deepening engagement and driving long-term loyalty.

Netflix, for example, continuously adapts its content strategy based on viewer data and feedback. By analyzing customer preferences and viewing habits, Netflix develops original content that appeals to its diverse user base. This customer-first approach has allowed Netflix to grow from a DVD rental service to a global streaming leader, maintaining strong customer loyalty even as competition has increased.

Brand elasticity: knowing when to stretch

Brand elasticity refers to how far your brand can stretch into new categories, markets, or products without losing its core identity. It's the balance between evolving to meet new market demands while maintaining the integrity of your brand's essence. Brands that stretch too far risk losing credibility, while those that don't stretch enough may become stagnant.

Coca-Cola has demonstrated strong brand elasticity by expanding its product line while maintaining its core identity as a beverage company. While Coca-Cola's flagship product remains its classic soda, the brand has successfully introduced products like flavored water, energy drinks, and health-conscious beverages to meet changing consumer preferences. This ability to stretch into new categories without diluting its core identity has helped Coca-Cola remain a leader in the beverage industry for over a century.

The key to brand elasticity is knowing how far to go. Brands need to ensure that any evolution or expansion aligns with their values and resonates with their audience. Stretching too far—into unrelated categories or markets—can confuse customers and weaken the brand.

The role of brand consistency in growth

Consistency is critical to building a brand that grows sustainably over time. While evolution and innovation are important, they must be grounded in a consistent brand message, tone, and identity. Customers need to recognize and trust the brand, even as it adapts and evolves. Brands that maintain consistency in their values, communication, and customer experience build a foundation of trust that drives loyalty and growth.

Starbucks is a prime example of a brand that has managed to evolve while staying consistent. Over the years, Starbucks has expanded globally, introduced new product lines, and integrated digital technology into its customer experience. However, through it all, the brand has remained consistent in its core message of offering a premium coffee experience, a focus on community, and a commitment to sustainability. This consistency, even amid growth and change, has helped Starbucks maintain its position as a global leader.

For brands, consistency doesn't mean resisting change—it means ensuring that change is in line with the brand's values and identity. By evolving strategically and staying true to their core, brands can grow while keeping their audience engaged and loyal.

Sustaining growth through brand loyalty

At the heart of sustained brand growth is customer loyalty. Brands that inspire loyalty through exceptional customer experiences, consistent values, and emotional connections are better positioned to weather market fluctuations and grow over time. Loyal customers not only provide a reliable revenue stream—they become advocates who help the brand expand organically through word-of-mouth and recommendations.

To build loyalty, brands need to focus on delivering value consistently. This means exceeding customer expectations, creating memorable experiences, and maintaining a strong emotional connection. Brands that invest in building and nurturing these relationships are more likely to see long-term success.

Measuring brand equity: evaluating your brand's market strength

Brand equity is a crucial metric for understanding the overall health and value of a brand in the marketplace. It reflects the power and perception a brand holds in the minds of consumers, which directly impacts customer loyalty, pricing power, and long-term growth. For businesses, measuring brand equity is key to ensuring that all efforts in branding, marketing, and customer experience are driving positive results and sustained market strength.

A strong brand equity allows companies to command higher prices, attract more loyal customers, and weather market challenges. But how do brands measure something as intangible as equity? There are specific strategies, metrics, and tools available to evaluate brand equity, providing valuable insights into how a brand is performing and what areas need attention.

What is brand equity?

Brand equity represents the added value a brand brings to a product or service. It's the reason why customers choose one brand over another, even when the product itself may be similar. Strong brand equity is built through a combination of factors, including brand awareness, customer perceptions, emotional connections, and consistent experiences.

Apple, for example, has one of the strongest brand equities in the world. The company's products often come at a premium, but consumers are willing to pay for the perceived innovation, design quality, and customer experience that Apple represents. This perception adds immense value to Apple's products, setting the company apart from competitors.

Brands with high equity enjoy stronger customer loyalty, better recognition, and a deeper emotional connection with their audience. They also benefit from a competitive advantage, as consumers are more likely to choose a trusted brand over an unknown one.

Methods for measuring brand equity

Measuring brand equity can be complex, as it involves both tangible and intangible factors. However, by using a combination of quantitative and qualitative approaches, brands can gain a clearer picture of their market strength and consumer perception.

1. Brand awareness

Brand awareness measures how well your target audience knows and recognizes your brand. It's one of the foundational elements of brand equity. High brand awareness means that your brand is top of mind when consumers are considering a purchase in your category.

Awareness can be measured through surveys, focus groups, or digital metrics like search volume, social media mentions, and website traffic. Tracking how often people think about or talk about your brand compared to competitors provides insight into your overall visibility in the market.

Brands like Coca-Cola, McDonald's, and Nike enjoy near-universal brand awareness, making them instantly recognizable and trusted across global markets. This widespread awareness contributes significantly to their overall brand equity.

2. Brand perception and customer sentiment

How customers perceive your brand—their feelings, opinions, and associations with it—plays a huge role in brand equity. Measuring brand perception helps you understand how your brand is viewed relative to your competitors and what emotional connections your customers feel. This emotional bond is often what separates strong brands from weak ones.

Surveys and social listening tools are effective ways to measure customer sentiment. Net Promoter Score (NPS) is a popular metric that measures how likely customers are to recommend your brand to others. A high NPS score indicates strong loyalty and positive brand perception, while a low score suggests room for improvement in customer satisfaction and brand advocacy.

Brands like Patagonia have built strong emotional equity through their environmental commitments and authentic values. Customers feel connected to Patagonia because it aligns with their own beliefs, making the brand more than just a product but a reflection of personal values.

3. Brand associations

Brand associations are the attributes, ideas, or emotions that people connect with your brand. These associations can be related to quality, luxury, sustainability, innovation, or other characteristics that define how your brand is perceived in the market. Understanding these associations helps you see what qualities customers link with your brand and how they compare to competitors.

For example, Mercedes-Benz is associated with luxury, prestige, and high-quality engineering, while Tesla is associated with innovation, sustainability, and cutting-edge technology. These associations play a key role in shaping brand equity.

To measure brand associations, brands often conduct qualitative research, such as focus groups, interviews, or customer surveys, asking people what comes to mind when they think of the brand. This helps brands understand how they are perceived and identify opportunities to strengthen or shift their positioning.

4. Brand loyalty

Customer loyalty is a critical component of brand equity. The more loyal your customers are, the stronger your brand equity will be. Loyal customers not only continue to purchase from your brand but also advocate for it, driving organic growth through word-of-mouth and social sharing.

Loyalty can be measured through repeat purchase rates, customer lifetime value (CLV), and customer retention rates. Additionally, brands can track engagement with loyalty programs or customer feedback to gauge how satisfied and committed customers are.

For instance, Starbucks has built a high level of customer loyalty through its *Starbucks Rewards* program, which encourages repeat purchases and long-term engagement. This loyalty translates into strong brand equity, as customers become advocates for the brand.

5. Financial performance and market share

A brand's financial performance is another way to measure brand equity. Strong brands tend to generate higher sales, command premium pricing, and capture significant market share. Analyzing revenue growth, profit margins, and market share in relation to competitors provides insight into how much of your financial success is driven by brand strength.

Brands with high equity, like Apple, can charge a premium for their products because customers perceive them as offering more value than cheaper alternatives. This pricing power, combined with a loyal customer base, is a key indicator of strong brand equity.

Measuring financial metrics like price elasticity—how price changes affect demand—can also reveal the strength of your brand equity. Brands with low price elasticity, meaning customers are less sensitive to price increases, tend to have higher brand equity because their customers see them as irreplaceable.

6. Customer feedback and reviews

Customer feedback, online reviews, and social media comments are powerful indicators of brand equity. Positive feedback and reviews suggest strong customer satisfaction and loyalty, while negative reviews may highlight areas where the brand is underperforming.

Monitoring online reviews through platforms like Google, Yelp, or Trustpilot, as well as engaging in social media listening, provides real-time insight into how customers feel about your brand. By tracking sentiment and identifying common themes in feedback, brands can address issues and leverage positive reviews to strengthen their brand equity.

Tesla, for instance, has built much of its brand equity through highly engaged customers who share their positive experiences across social media platforms, fueling both loyalty and brand advocacy.

The role of consistency in building brand equity

Consistency is crucial when it comes to maintaining and growing brand equity. Brands that deliver a consistent experience across all touchpoints—whether through messaging, customer service, or product quality—build trust with their customers. This trust translates into higher loyalty, stronger emotional connections, and, ultimately, more robust brand equity.

Coca-Cola's brand equity is rooted in its consistent global identity. No matter where you are in the world, the red-and-white branding, familiar logo, and signature taste remain the same. This consistency helps Coca-Cola maintain its position as one of the most valuable brands globally, regardless of market fluctuations.

Using brand equity insights to drive growth

Once you have a clear understanding of your brand's equity, you can use these insights to refine your marketing strategies, improve customer experiences, and strengthen your market position. If your brand awareness is low, you might invest more in visibility campaigns. If your brand perception is lagging, you may need to focus on improving customer satisfaction or repositioning your brand to align with customer values.

Tracking brand equity over time allows you to see how your efforts are paying off and where you need to pivot to maintain growth. By continually measuring and improving your brand's equity, you ensure that your brand remains strong, relevant, and competitive in the long term.

Adapting to market trends: the role of flexibility in brand evolution

In a rapidly changing marketplace, the ability to adapt to trends and evolving consumer behaviors is crucial to a brand's long-term success. Markets are constantly shifting due to technological advances, economic fluctuations, and shifts in consumer expectations. Brands that remain rigid and fail to evolve risk becoming irrelevant, while those that embrace flexibility are more likely to thrive.

Flexibility in brand evolution doesn't mean abandoning core values or constantly reinventing your identity. It's about adapting to external changes while staying true to what makes your brand unique. Brands that strike this balance can remain competitive, meet customer needs, and continue to grow even in unpredictable environments.

Why flexibility matters in brand evolution

Flexibility allows brands to stay relevant as trends, technologies, and consumer preferences shift. Brands that successfully adapt to these changes build resilience and are better equipped to navigate market challenges. While it's important to maintain consistency in your brand identity, it's equally important to evolve in response to external pressures and opportunities.

Netflix is a perfect example of a brand that has embraced flexibility. What started as a DVD rental service has transformed into a global streaming giant, adapting to technological changes and consumer demand for on-demand content. By pivoting from its original business model, Netflix not only survived but thrived in a rapidly evolving industry. Its ability to adapt to the rise of digital streaming and then expand into content production and original programming demonstrates the power of flexibility in brand evolution.

Without flexibility, brands risk becoming stagnant. As consumer expectations change, especially with the rise of digital experiences, brands that fail to evolve may lose their competitive edge. Flexibility allows for innovation, experimentation, and adaptation—all key ingredients for sustained growth.

The importance of monitoring market trends

To stay ahead of the curve, brands need to be proactive in monitoring market trends. This includes staying informed about industry shifts, emerging technologies, and changes in consumer behavior. Brands that actively track and respond to trends can adapt more quickly, positioning themselves as leaders rather than followers in their industry.

A great example is the rise of sustainability as a key consumer value. In recent years, brands across industries have had to adjust their practices and messaging to align with growing consumer demand for environmentally responsible products. Companies like Unilever have embraced this shift, integrating sustainability into their long-term strategy and making it a core part of their brand identity. By monitoring consumer trends and pivoting towards eco-friendly initiatives, Unilever has maintained relevance while appealing to a new generation of environmentally conscious consumers.

Tools like social media monitoring, consumer surveys, and market research reports can provide valuable insights into emerging trends. By staying informed, brands can make strategic decisions about where to innovate, which trends to follow, and how to align their evolution with what matters most to their customers.

Staying customer-focused during change

While it's important to adapt to market trends, brands must always remain customer-centric. Brands that lose sight of their core audience while chasing trends can risk alienating loyal customers. Successful brand evolution requires balancing adaptation with the needs, preferences, and values of your customer base.

Take Starbucks, for example. As consumer tastes shifted towards healthier options, Starbucks introduced alternative milk options, plant-based food items, and low-calorie drink choices to meet changing preferences. However, it did so without losing the essence of what made Starbucks a community-focused brand centered around the coffee experience. By evolving its menu to reflect customer preferences while maintaining its core identity, Starbucks has continued to attract new customers without sacrificing loyalty from its existing base.

When adapting to trends, brands must ensure that changes align with their values and the expectations of their audience. Customers who feel that a brand's evolution reflects their own needs and values are more likely to remain loyal, even as the brand innovates.

Innovation as a key to adaptation

Innovation is central to adapting to market trends. Brands that invest in research and development, product innovation, and technology are better equipped to meet new demands and seize opportunities. By fostering a culture of innovation, brands can stay ahead of the curve and continually find new ways to deliver value to their customers.

Tesla is a brand that has built its reputation on constant innovation. From electric vehicles to advancements in battery technology and autonomous driving, Tesla continually pushes the boundaries of what's possible in the automotive industry. This commitment to innovation has allowed Tesla to not only adapt to but also lead the market trend towards sustainable, eco-friendly transportation.

However, innovation isn't just about product development—it can also be about enhancing the customer experience, improving operational efficiency, or finding new ways to engage with your audience. For example, companies that have embraced digital transformation by creating seamless online shopping experiences, personalized marketing, and enhanced mobile apps have successfully adapted to the rise of e-commerce and changing consumer expectations.

Knowing when to pivot and when to stay the course

Flexibility in brand evolution also requires knowing when to pivot and when to stay the course. Not every trend is worth following, and not every shift in the market requires a major change. Successful brands understand when a trend aligns with their values and long-term vision and when it doesn't.

For example, while many companies have jumped on the influencer marketing trend, some luxury brands have taken a more cautious approach, recognizing that over-commercialization could dilute their brand's exclusivity. Brands like Hermès and Chanel have remained selective in their partnerships, focusing on maintaining their high-end image rather than chasing social media trends that could conflict with their carefully crafted identity.

Brands that know when to pivot based on market opportunities, without losing sight of their core identity, are more likely to achieve long-term success. It's important to evaluate whether a trend fits your brand's positioning and how it will impact your relationship with your customers.

Balancing tradition with innovation

For heritage brands or brands with a long history, balancing tradition with innovation can be a delicate task. While these brands have built equity on consistency, legacy, and reliability, they must also evolve to remain relevant in a fast-changing market. Successfully blending tradition with innovation allows brands to honor their past while embracing the future.

Take BMW, for example. The brand is rooted in tradition, with a long history of producing luxury vehicles known for their engineering and performance. However, BMW has also embraced electric vehicles and sustainable practices, introducing the BMW i Series to appeal to environmentally conscious consumers. By innovating without losing sight of its core identity as a luxury performance brand, BMW has maintained its relevance in the competitive automotive industry.

Brands that have a strong heritage need to be mindful of how they evolve, ensuring that changes resonate with their existing customers while attracting new ones. Balancing tradition with innovation requires thoughtful, strategic decisions that reflect both the brand's legacy and its vision for the future.

Flexibility in brand communication

Adapting to market trends also requires flexibility in brand communication. As new platforms emerge, and as consumer attention shifts from traditional media to digital spaces, brands need to adapt their messaging and communication strategies to remain relevant and engaging.

Brands like Nike have mastered this shift, leveraging digital platforms, social media, and influencer partnerships to communicate with younger, tech-savvy audiences while maintaining their core message of empowerment and athleticism. Nike's *Just Do It* campaign, for example, has evolved across multiple platforms, from TV commercials to Instagram campaigns and YouTube series, all while maintaining consistency in its message and identity.

Flexibility in communication also involves adjusting the tone, style, and approach to fit the platform while keeping the brand voice consistent. Whether engaging through short-form video content on TikTok or long-form thought leadership pieces on LinkedIn, successful brands know how to tailor their communication to suit the platform without compromising their identity.

Navigating crises with flexibility

In addition to responding to market trends, flexibility is essential in navigating unexpected crises or disruptions. Whether it's an economic downturn, a global pandemic, or a sudden shift in consumer sentiment, brands that can pivot quickly are better positioned to manage challenges and continue growing.

The COVID-19 pandemic forced many brands to rethink their strategies and operations. Those that were flexible enough to shift to e-commerce, offer digital services, or adapt their messaging to reflect the new reality were able to weather the storm better than those that stuck to pre-pandemic strategies. For example, fitness brands like Peloton thrived by offering at-home workout solutions, while restaurants pivoted to delivery and takeout models.

By being flexible in times of crisis, brands can not only survive but also strengthen their relationship with customers by demonstrating responsiveness, resilience, and adaptability.

Staying relevant: how brands evolve to meet consumer expectations

In an era where consumer preferences are constantly changing, brands that want to remain competitive must evolve alongside their audience. Staying relevant is not just about keeping up with trends but about anticipating shifts in customer expectations and continuously refining how the brand delivers value. Consumers today are more informed, more connected, and more demanding than ever, and brands that fail to adapt risk being left behind.

To stay relevant, brands must evolve in ways that align with their core values while embracing innovation, new technologies, and the changing cultural landscape. It's a delicate balance of holding onto what makes the brand unique and staying flexible enough to pivot when consumer needs evolve.

Understanding evolving consumer expectations

The first step in staying relevant is understanding the evolving needs and expectations of your audience. Consumer expectations are shaped by a variety of factors, including technological advancements, social and environmental awareness, and cultural shifts. Brands need to stay ahead of these changes by continuously listening to their customers and monitoring broader market trends.

For example, sustainability has become a major expectation for many consumers, particularly among younger generations. Brands that integrate sustainable practices into their operations, products, and messaging are seen as more responsible and forward-thinking. Companies like Patagonia have long embraced sustainability as a core part of their brand identity, but more recently, even fast-fashion retailers like H&M have begun shifting towards more sustainable practices to meet consumer demand.

Understanding these shifts requires ongoing engagement with your audience, including gathering feedback through surveys, focus groups, and social media monitoring. Brands that invest in understanding their customers are better positioned to anticipate changes and adapt their offerings accordingly.

The role of innovation in staying relevant

Innovation is one of the most important factors in staying relevant. Brands that embrace innovation not only meet consumer expectations but also set the pace for change in their industry. Whether through product development, customer experience enhancements, or digital transformation, innovation keeps a brand fresh and exciting.

Take Nike, for example. Known for constantly pushing the boundaries of athletic wear, Nike has maintained its relevance by continuously innovating. Whether it's through technological advancements like the self-lacing *Nike Adapt* shoes or by integrating digital tools such as the *Nike Training Club* app, Nike constantly meets consumer expectations for performance, technology, and convenience. Innovation ensures that Nike remains at the forefront of consumer demand for both function and style.

Innovation doesn't have to mean large-scale, industry-disrupting changes. Incremental improvements, such as introducing new product features, enhancing customer service, or improving digital interfaces, can also keep a brand relevant. By continually improving and evolving, brands can meet customer expectations for convenience, personalization, and quality.

Flexibility in brand positioning

Staying relevant often means adjusting your brand's positioning to meet the needs of a changing market. Flexibility in how you communicate your brand's value, purpose, and benefits is key to ensuring that your brand resonates with current and potential customers. However, it's important to evolve your positioning without losing the essence of what your brand stands for.

One brand that has successfully adapted its positioning to remain relevant is Dove. Dove's original focus was on skincare and soap products, but the brand has evolved into a leader in body positivity and women's empowerment. Through campaigns like *Real Beauty*, Dove shifted its positioning to focus on self-esteem and inclusivity, aligning its messaging with cultural conversations around beauty standards. This shift allowed Dove to stay relevant by addressing a broader societal issue while still selling its core products.

Brands that can adapt their positioning to align with cultural or social movements while maintaining their authenticity are more likely to remain relevant in a fast-changing landscape.

Delivering a consistent and personalized customer experience

Consumers today expect more than just good products; they expect an experience that feels personal, relevant, and consistent across all touchpoints. To meet these expectations, brands must invest in delivering seamless and personalized customer experiences, whether online or in-store. Personalization can take many forms, from tailored marketing messages to customized product recommendations or personalized customer support.

Amazon is one of the most notable examples of a brand that has perfected the art of personalization. By using customer data to provide personalized product recommendations, customized marketing emails, and tailored shopping experiences, Amazon ensures that its customers feel like each interaction is unique. This personalization not only meets customer expectations but also creates a sense of loyalty and engagement that keeps customers coming back.

At the same time, consistency across touchpoints is critical. Whether a customer is browsing your website, interacting on social media, or visiting a physical store, the brand experience should feel cohesive. Consistency reinforces trust and helps ensure that customers know what to expect from the brand, no matter how they choose to engage with it.

Responsiveness to social and cultural movements

Staying relevant today requires brands to be in tune with social and cultural movements. Consumers, particularly younger generations, expect the brands they support to take a stand on important social issues, whether it's environmental sustainability, diversity and inclusion, or corporate responsibility. Brands that ignore these expectations risk being perceived as out of touch, while those that respond in authentic and meaningful ways can build stronger connections with their audience.

Ben & Jerry's is an example of a brand that has built its identity around social activism. From climate change to racial justice, Ben & Jerry's has consistently taken a stand on important social issues, integrating these values into its brand messaging and marketing campaigns. This approach not only aligns with consumer expectations but also differentiates the brand from competitors who may shy away from addressing controversial topics.

For brands, the key is authenticity. Consumers can easily spot brands that are jumping on the bandwagon versus those that are genuinely committed to the causes they support. Brands that respond authentically to social and cultural movements are more likely to build long-term loyalty and trust.

Staying relevant through digital transformation

In a world increasingly driven by technology, digital transformation is essential for staying relevant. Brands that embrace digital tools, from e-commerce platforms to AI-powered customer support, can deliver faster, more efficient, and more personalized experiences that meet today's consumer expectations. This shift is especially important as more consumers move online for shopping, entertainment, and communication.

Brands like Sephora have embraced digital transformation by creating a seamless omnichannel experience. Sephora's app allows customers to virtually try on makeup, access personalized product recommendations, and make purchases. In-store, customers can use digital tools to check inventory, book appointments, and receive personalized advice. By integrating digital technology into both online and offline experiences, Sephora meets consumer expectations for convenience, personalization, and innovation.

Digital transformation is not just about adopting new technology—it's about using technology to enhance the customer experience and create new ways for consumers to interact with your brand. By staying digitally agile, brands can keep up with shifting expectations and remain relevant in an increasingly digital world.

The importance of agility and continuous improvement

Perhaps the most critical factor in staying relevant is agility. Brands must be able to pivot quickly in response to changing trends, new technologies, and evolving consumer expectations. This requires a mindset of continuous improvement, where brands are always looking for ways to innovate, refine their offerings, and enhance the customer experience.

Brands that adopt an agile approach are better equipped to navigate uncertainty and capitalize on emerging opportunities. For example, during the COVID-19 pandemic, many brands had to quickly shift their strategies to accommodate changing consumer behaviors, such as the increased demand for online shopping and contactless delivery. Brands like Target successfully adapted by ramping up their e-commerce capabilities, offering curbside pickup, and enhancing their digital presence, all while maintaining the core elements of their brand identity.

Agility doesn't just apply to external market changes—it also means regularly assessing and refining internal processes. Brands that embrace a culture of agility and innovation are better positioned to adapt and grow in the face of evolving consumer expectations.

Looking ahead: evolving with purpose

As consumer expectations continue to evolve, staying relevant means evolving with purpose. Brands that want to remain competitive must approach change strategically, ensuring that every pivot, innovation, and new direction aligns with their core values and long-term vision. Evolution is not about following every trend—it's about making thoughtful, purpose-driven decisions that strengthen the brand's relationship with its customers.

Ultimately, staying relevant requires brands to remain deeply connected to their audience, invest in innovation, and stay agile in the face of change. Brands that evolve thoughtfully and authentically will be better positioned to meet future challenges and continue delivering value to their customers over time.

CONCLUSION

The ongoing journey of brand-building

Final thoughts on using this framework to future-proof your brand

The 6 E's of Branding framework offers more than just a step-by-step guide to building a successful brand—it provides a roadmap for navigating the complexities of an ever-changing marketplace. By integrating the principles of Exploration, Essence, Expression, Experience, Engagement, and Evolution, brands can stay flexible, relevant, and resilient, even as consumer preferences and industry landscapes shift.

At its core, this framework is about building a brand that is not only strong in the present but also equipped to thrive in the future. By focusing on discovery and understanding your brand's unique identity, creating meaningful and consistent experiences, and maintaining deep connections with your audience, your brand becomes future-proof, ready to adapt to whatever challenges or opportunities come next.

Brands that rely solely on past successes are at risk of being disrupted, but those that continually evolve, innovate, and stay connected to their customers are more likely to sustain long-term growth. This framework provides the tools and insights necessary for businesses to remain competitive and agile, no matter what changes come their way.

Whether you're launching a new brand or looking to refine an established one, using this framework will ensure that your brand remains authentic, adaptable, and aligned with the values of your audience. It helps you build a brand that isn't just reactive to trends but proactive in shaping its future, turning loyal customers into lifelong advocates.

By following these principles, you can create a brand that not only meets the challenges of today but also anticipates the needs of tomorrow. The key to future-proofing your brand is staying true to your essence while embracing the flexibility required to grow and evolve with your market.

The power of evolving brands

By mastering the art of discovery in the *Exploration* phase, brands can ensure they are built on a foundation of insights, understanding both their competitive landscape and the needs of their audience. Through defining their *Essence*, brands can articulate a clear identity that resonates with consumers and sets them apart in crowded markets. In the *Expression* phase, brands bring this identity to life through visual and verbal cues that communicate who they are, ensuring consistency across all touchpoints.

Building strong *Experiences* deepens customer loyalty and transforms transactions into emotional connections, while *Engagement* fosters relationships that turn customers into advocates. Finally, embracing *Evolution* allows brands to adapt, innovate, and stay relevant in an ever-changing landscape, ensuring sustained growth and market leadership.

As you apply this framework to your own brand, remember that every brand's journey is unique, but the principles remain the same. By staying true to your brand's core values while remaining open to change and innovation, you can build a brand that stands the test of time. A brand that not only captures attention but also wins hearts—and ultimately, shapes the future.

APPENDIX
Branding Glossary

1. Brand
A brand is more than just a name, logo, or visual identity; it represents the total perception of a company, product, or service in the minds of consumers. It encompasses everything from customer experience and values to emotional connections.

2. Brand Architecture
The strategic organization of a company's brands, products, and services within its portfolio. Common models include branded house (e.g., Google) and house of brands (e.g., Procter & Gamble).

3. Brand Awareness
The extent to which consumers recognize or recall a brand. High brand awareness means that a brand is top-of-mind when consumers are considering a purchase in its category.

4. Brand Community
A group of consumers who are emotionally invested in a brand and who engage with each other around shared interests or values related to that brand. A strong brand community can drive customer loyalty and advocacy.

5. Brand Consistency
The practice of ensuring that a brand's messaging, tone, and visual elements are uniform across all platforms and touchpoints, creating a cohesive and recognizable identity.

6. Brand Equity
The value that a brand adds to a product or service beyond its functional benefits. Brand equity is built through consumer trust, loyalty, and positive associations, often leading to pricing power and competitive advantage.

7. Brand Essence
The core of a brand's identity, often expressed in a simple phrase or idea that captures its purpose, values, and personality. The essence should be reflected in every aspect of the brand's communication and experience.

8. Brand Experience
The cumulative impact of all interactions a consumer has with a brand, from marketing communications to customer service, product use, and beyond. A seamless brand experience fosters loyalty and emotional connections.

9. Brand Expression
How a brand's identity is visually and verbally communicated through logos, taglines, colors, messaging, and tone of voice. Consistency in brand expression reinforces brand recognition and trust.

10. Brand Extension
The practice of leveraging an established brand name to enter a new product category. Successful brand extensions build on the brand's core strengths, while poorly aligned extensions can dilute brand equity.

11. Brand Identity
The visual and verbal components that distinguish a brand in the marketplace. This includes logos, colors, fonts, tone of voice, and overall messaging, all of which should align with the brand's core values and positioning.

12. Brand Loyalty
A consumer's commitment to repeatedly purchase or support a specific brand, often driven by emotional attachment and satisfaction. Loyal customers tend to advocate for the brand, making loyalty a key driver of long-term success.

13. Brand Personality
The human characteristics and traits that are attributed to a brand, such as

being innovative, friendly, or luxurious. These traits help consumers relate to the brand on an emotional level.

14. Brand Positioning
The process of defining a brand's place in the market, relative to competitors, based on unique value propositions and attributes that resonate with the target audience. Strong positioning creates differentiation and appeal.

15. Brand Promise
The value or experience a brand consistently delivers to its customers. The promise is the brand's commitment to meet or exceed consumer expectations and is crucial to building trust and loyalty.

16. Brand Relevance
The degree to which a brand's offerings align with the needs, desires, and values of its target audience. Brands that stay relevant evolve alongside their customers and market trends.

17. Brand Story
The narrative that communicates a brand's mission, values, and history, often used to create an emotional connection with consumers. A compelling brand story differentiates a brand from competitors and humanizes it in the eyes of consumers.

18. Brand Stretch
The ability of a brand to extend into new product categories or markets without losing its core identity. Successful brand stretching requires staying true to the brand's essence while adapting to new opportunities.

19. Brand Voice
The unique tone and style of communication that a brand uses to connect with its audience. Consistency in brand voice reinforces brand identity and helps build a strong emotional connection with consumers.

20. Brand Equity Measurement
The process of evaluating a brand's overall strength in the market, typically using metrics like brand awareness, customer loyalty, market share, and financial performance.

21. Brand Touchpoints
The various interactions a consumer has with a brand across different platforms and channels, such as websites, social media, in-store experi-

ences, and customer service. Each touchpoint contributes to the overall brand experience.

22. Customer Journey
The full lifecycle of interactions a customer has with a brand, from initial awareness to post-purchase experience and advocacy. Mapping the customer journey helps brands create meaningful engagement at every stage.

23. Customer-Centricity
A business approach focused on creating positive experiences for the customer by understanding and addressing their needs, desires, and pain points. Brands that are customer-centric often enjoy stronger loyalty and advocacy.

24. Differentiation
The process of distinguishing a brand from its competitors by highlighting unique attributes, benefits, or features. Effective differentiation helps brands stand out and attract the attention of their target audience.

25. Emotional Branding
A strategy that focuses on building a strong emotional connection between a brand and its customers, often through storytelling, brand experiences, and values alignment. Brands that evoke positive emotions create lasting loyalty.

26. Employer Branding
The practice of creating and promoting a company's reputation as an employer. A strong employer brand attracts top talent and fosters employee loyalty, which in turn contributes to the brand's overall success.

27. Engagement
The level of interaction and involvement a customer has with a brand, whether through social media, customer service, loyalty programs, or brand events. High engagement often correlates with stronger customer loyalty and advocacy.

28. Rebranding
The process of altering a brand's identity, positioning, or messaging to reflect a new direction, market opportunity, or cultural shift. Rebranding is often used to modernize or refresh a brand but can be risky if not managed carefully.

29. Sensory Branding
The use of multi-sensory cues—sight, sound, touch, taste, and smell—to create a more immersive brand experience. Engaging multiple senses strengthens emotional connections and improves brand recall.

30. Visual Identity
The visual components of a brand, including its logo, colors, typography, and imagery. A consistent and compelling visual identity helps reinforce brand recognition and supports overall branding efforts.

REFERENCES

Aaker, D. A. (1991). *Managing brand equity: Capitalizing on the value of a brand name*. Free Press.

Aaker, D. A. (1996). *Building strong brands*. Free Press.

Batra, R., Ahuvia, A., & Bagozzi, R. P. (2012). Brand love. *Journal of Marketing*, 76(2), 1-16. https://doi.org/10.1509/jm.09.0339

Belk, R. W. (1988). Possessions and the extended self. *Journal of Consumer Research*, 15(2), 139-168. https://doi.org/10.1086/209154

Berthon, P., Hulbert, J. M., & Pitt, L. F. (1999). Brand management prognostications. *Sloan Management Review*, 40(2), 53-65. https://sloanreview.mit.edu/article/brand-management-prognostications/

Beverland, M. B. (2005). Crafting brand authenticity: The case of luxury wines. *Journal of Management Studies*, 42(5), 1003-1029. https://doi.org/10.1111/j.1467-6486.2005.00531.x

Burmann, C., Jost-Benz, M., & Riley, N. (2009). Towards an identity-based brand equity model. *Journal of Business Research*, 62(3), 390-397. https://doi.org/10.1016/j.jbusres.2008.06.009

Chandon, P., Hutchinson, J. W., Bradlow, E. T., & Young, S. H. (2009). Does in-store marketing work? Effects of the number and position of shelf facings on brand attention and evaluation at the point of purchase. *Journal of Marketing*, 73(6), 1-17. https://doi.org/10.1509/jmkg.73.6.1

Christodoulides, G., & de Chernatony, L. (2010). Consumer-based brand equity conceptualization and measurement: A literature review. *International Journal of Market Research*, 52(1), 43-66. https://doi.org/10.2501/S1470785310201053

De Mooij, M. (2010). *Global marketing and advertising: Understanding cultural paradoxes* (3rd ed.). Sage Publications.

Erdem, T., & Swait, J. (1998). Brand equity as a signaling phenomenon. *Journal of Consumer Psychology*, 7(2), 131-157. https://doi.org/10.1207/s15327663jcp0702_02

Fournier, S. (1998). Consumers and their brands: Developing relationship theory in consumer research. *Journal of Consumer Research*, 24(4), 343-373. https://doi.org/10.1086/209515

Holt, D. B. (2004). *How brands become icons: The principles of cultural branding*. Harvard Business School Press.

Kapferer, J. N. (2012). *The new strategic brand management: Advanced insights and strategic thinking* (5th ed.). Kogan Page.

Keller, K. L. (1993). Conceptualizing, measuring, and managing customer-based brand equity. *Journal of Marketing*, 57(1), 1-22. https://doi.org/10.2307/1252054

Keller, K. L. (2009). Building strong brands in a modern marketing communications environment. *Journal of Marketing Communications*, 15(2-3), 139-155. https://doi.org/10.1080/13527260902757530

Kotler, P., & Keller, K. L. (2016). *Marketing management* (15th ed.). Pearson.

Krishna, A. (2012). An integrative review of sensory marketing: Engaging the senses to affect perception, judgment, and behavior. *Journal of Consumer Psychology*, 22(3), 332-351. https://doi.org/10.1016/j.jcps.2011.08.003

Lemon, K. N., & Verhoef, P. C. (2016). Understanding customer experience throughout the customer journey. *Journal of Marketing*, 80(6), 69-96. https://doi.org/10.1509/jm.15.0420

Matzler, K., Grabner-Kräuter, S., & Bidmon, S. (2008). Risk aversion and brand loyalty: The mediating role of brand trust and brand affect. *Journal of Product & Brand Management*, 17(3), 154-162. https://doi.org/10.1108/10610420810875070

Morhart, F. M., Malär, L., Guèvremont, A., Girardin, F., & Grohmann, B. (2015). Brand authenticity: An integrative framework and measurement scale. *Journal of Consumer Psychology*, 25(2), 200-218. https://doi.org/10.1016/j.jcps.2014.11.006

Neumeier, M. (2006). *The brand gap: How to bridge the distance between business strategy and design*. New Riders.

Park, C. W., Jaworski, B. J., & MacInnis, D. J. (1986). Strategic brand concept-image management. *Journal of Marketing*, 50(4), 135-145. https://doi.org/10.1177/002224298605000401

Ries, A., & Trout, J. (2001). *Positioning: The battle for your mind* (20th ed.). McGraw-Hill.

Schmitt, B. (1999). Experiential marketing. *Journal of Marketing Management*, 15(1-3), 53-67. https://doi.org/10.1362/026725799784870496

Smith, R. E., & Park, W. C. (1992). The effects of brand extensions on market share and advertising efficiency. *Journal of Marketing Research*, 29(3), 296-313. https://doi.org/10.2307/3172741

Yoo, B., Donthu, N., & Lee, S. (2000). An examination of selected marketing mix elements and brand equity. *Journal of the Academy of Marketing Science*, 28(2), 195-211. https://doi.org/10.1177/0092070300282002

THANK YOU

Marcos G. Figueira
Instagram
@marcosfigueira
LinkedIn
@marcosfigueira

Marcia Berardinelli
Instagram
@marciaberardinellidefreitas
LinkedIn
@marcia-berardinelli

http://marcosfigueira.com
https://wyse.com.br

www.ingramcontent.com/pod-product-compliance
Lightning Source LLC
Chambersburg PA
CBHW052158220526
45471CB00004B/1719